I Just Lost Myself

I JUST LOST MYSELF

Psychological Abuse of Women in Marriage

Valerie Nash Chang

Westport, Connecticut
London

Library of Congress Cataloging-in-Publication Data

Chang, Valerie Nash.
    I just lost myself : psychological abuse of women in marriage /
Valerie Nash Chang.
        p.   cm.
    Includes bibliographical references and index.
    ISBN 0–275–95209–6 (alk. paper)
        1.   Wife abuse—United States.   2. Wife abuse—United States—
Psychological aspects.   3. Women—United States—Psychology.
I. Title.
HV6626.22.U6C48   1996
362.82'92—dc20   95–30660

British Library Cataloguing in Publication Data is available.

Library of Congress Catalog Card Number: 95–30660
ISBN: 0–275–95209–6

First published in 1996

Praeger Publishers, 88 Post Road West, Westport, CT 06881
An imprint of Greenwood Publishing Group, Inc.

Printed in the United States of America

∞™

The paper used in this book complies with the
Permanent Paper Standard issued by the National
Information Standards Organziation (Z39.48–1984).

10 9 8 7 6 5 4 3

For my parents,
Howard and Ava Nash,
who always believed I could do it.

CONTENTS

ACKNOWLEDGMENTS

This book would not have been possible without the women participants who shared their stories with me. I am very grateful for the depth and wealth of information they gave me. They are truly remarkable women and I thank each one.

This is a study of women, and there is a long list of women to thank. The first influential woman in my life was my mother, an energetic, enthusiastic, positive person who knows she can do whatever she sets her mind to do and expects no less from her daughter. I have also been lucky to know many other powerful, capable women whose lives have affected mine: Jacqui Schiff, Emily Ruppert, Petruska Clarkson, Sue Fish, Muriel James, Mary Ellen Frost, and Eleanor Turk, to name a few. Joy Holthouse, my secretary and good friend for years, typed all the transcripts. Sandy Augustin has been calm, steady, and accepting through all the ups and downs of the past several years. Early in this project, my good friend, Ann Hanson, helped me with typing, cooking, and many other things. My daughter, Amy Hinshaw, not only offered many fine suggestions for making the summary more easily readable, but also is a model of the new generation of women who highly value their uniqueness and maintain their power while establishing close relationships.

Maggie Blay, Judy Kline, Liza Hyatt, Cindy Rice, Nancy White, Rose Howard, and Tina Grimberg—the wonderful psychotherapists at the Julian Center—told women about this project and discussed it with me. Margaret Adamek was a great help and supporter of the project; she is a terrific editor who has spent hours carefully reading drafts and asking thought-provoking questions, which invited me to develop my ideas. Eileen Cantin and Yvonne Williams, who have been colleagues for years, supported this project by discussing it with me and telling psychologically abused clients about it. Sally Randolph, from the Authors Guild, spent hours teaching me about publishing contracts. My editor, Liz Murphy, and everyone at Greenwood Publishing have been helpful through the complex process of getting this book published. And, of course, each of the women I've worked with over the years has taught me something and expanded my understanding of women today.

I also want to acknowledge the support and help of many folks from the other gender. Dinner table debates with my father taught me analytical and critical thinking, a gift for which I have often been grateful. George Zirkle and Jack McCrary were college professors who always seemed to have the right challenge to push me beyond what I thought I could do. Hedges Capers, a clinical supervisor, saw my ability as a psychotherapist and my personal capacity to create a different life story than the one I had learned. My colleague, John Rife, carried a tremendous work load one year so that I could take a one year sabbatical leave to begin the work that led to this project. Norm Denzin supported this project from the beginning, often providing suggestions, different perspectives, and encouragement. Chuck Cowger helped me back when my ideas were only vaguely defined. My colleague, Dale Sauer, referred a woman to the study and loaned me his office to meet with her. Steve Miller's support included connecting me with leaders of two Divorce Recovery groups, letting me use space in the church, and having faith that the project was important and could be accomplished by me. My dear friend, Stan Stackhouse, proofread every chapter and was patient and accepting during long periods when all my energy went into this project. My son and son-in-law, Jeff Chang and James Hinshaw, offer hope that young men want equal relationships with women they respect. The support and ideas of each of these wonderful people has been very important to me in my life and critical to the completion of this project.

There are also many people at Indiana University who helped

me along the way, particularly my colleagues at Indiana University East and at Indiana University School of Social Work. The School of Journalism and School of Education even helped out toward the end of the project.

A COMMENT ON LANGUAGE

For at least half of my life, I lived with a gendered language system that used universal male pronouns. Finally this system gave way to the still-gendered and awkward he/she, him/her; but no neutral first-person pronoun has been developed. As a protest and a preference, I will use a universal female pronoun to refer to she/he in hopes that, if enough people call attention to this problem, our language structure will somehow change and individuals will be thought of as individuals without forced reference to gender.

I Just Lost Myself

INTRODUCTION

> I think I could be the wife he wants, but when I try to do that I lose so much of me that I become depressed. If I try to get him to understand my side, he says that I am being selfish and then leaves. It doesn't matter what I do, I end up depressed. (40 year old teacher)

This woman is describing her experience in a psychologically abusive marriage. The process involved him using excessive demands, threats, dominating behavior, and criticism in an attempt to control her. If she responded defensively, he became angrier and either threatened to leave or left. Feeling frightened by his anger and threats and wanting to please him, she generally adapted submissively in an attempt to end the conflict and create peace. As she continued to adapt, she lost touch with her unique sense of self and became depressed. This process was described by the other women I interviewed.

In this book, I put these women's narratives in context; their vivid reports describe and explain psychological abuse. Their life stories are courageous journeys of moving out of one reality, one style of thinking and being, into a new reality. Their hope is that their experiences will inform others who want to increase their understanding of psychological abuse.

Shortly after I decided to study psychological abuse of women in marriage, three women in one of my therapy groups were talking about what to do about marriages that were very painful. One woman worked intensely on trying to figure out what held her in her painful marriage. She knew all the rational reasons for leaving the marriage and had been advised by many people that she should leave. She had also gotten beyond her fears of living alone, yet she still stayed. Why? Why did this attractive, competent, and capable woman stay in this emotionally damaging marriage? I could describe psychological abuse but did not understand it. A review of the available literature provided little information. One of my colleagues said that she thought some of her women clients stayed in emotionally destructive marriages because they felt obligated to take care of their husbands and were unwilling to do anything that might be hurtful to the men even though they were abusive. That explanation made sense but seemed incomplete. Did women stay in psychologically abusive relationships for the same reasons that kept women in physically abusive relationships? How were these two types of abuse similar and how different?

Although I have heard many women talk about psychological abuse in marriage, I had many unanswered questions about these relationships. Did they have common interaction patterns and themes? Were there similar turning points for women in these relationships? What impact did ongoing psychological abuse have on the lives of women? When in the relationship did personal shifts take place? These are some of the many questions that drove my study of psychological abuse in marriage.

Unfortunately, the issue of psychological abuse has received little attention except as an aspect of physically abusive relationships (see, for example, Ferraro 1979; Follingstad et al. 1990; Tolman 1989, 1992; Walker 1979). Maybe we are still trying to protect the image of the family and do not want to face even more abuse. Certainly, as a clinician and educator, I did not want to hear about more abuse of women; but I knew I would hear more, and I believed that additional research on the process of change in psychologically abusive relationships would be helpful to many women. I have had considerable experience with psychologically abusive relationships and I am sure that knowledge about this phenomenon will be very useful to psychotherapists and to the women who are struggling to understand abusive relationships. I know that as a result of this study I hear about psychological abuse with more understanding and act with more compassion.

In my search to understand psychological abuse, I used many sources. The research that came from studying the psychological abuse in physically abusive relationships provided the foundation for my study (e.g., Ferraro 1979; Tolman 1989, 1992; Walker 1979). I also reviewed the ideas contained in recent popular psychology literature on aspects of psychological abuse (Engels 1990; Evans 1992; Forward 1986).

The information in this book combines material from studies of psychological abuse within physically abusive relationships and studies of characteristics of psychological abuse (e.g., Stets 1991; Tolman 1992), with data from my study of women who had been in or are in psychologically abusive relationships. My study (Chang 1994) focused on descriptions of experience, perceptions, and process and was oriented to understanding unique but frequently occurring phenomena (Glaser and Strauss 1967; Reinharz 1979).

Although discovering "objective reality" about all women is not possible, it is possible to listen to women's descriptions of their external and internal realities and their perceptions of their experiences (Jack 1991). From these descriptions, an understanding of how women experience psychological abuse emerged. Certainly there are differences related to factors such as age, ethnicity, race, religion, socioeconomic class, and education; but the basic characteristics of the relationship and its evolution are very similar.

INTERPRETING LIFE STORIES

Since my goal was understanding the feelings, experiences, thoughts, and process of change in the women who have experienced psychological abuse, I used an interpretative interactionism method of study (Denzin 1989a). An interpretative method is one that studies the processes used to make sense of and give meaning to reality (Bateson 1972; Goffman 1974). These processes involve a self-narrative, which is the person's account of the important events in her life (Gergen and Gergen 1984; Robinson and Hawpe 1986). Self-narratives arrange experiences in order and sequence over time, explain causation, give meaning to personal events, and make sense of personal experience (Bruner 1986; Gergen and Gergen 1984; Polkinghorne 1988; Riessman 1990; Robinson and Hawpe 1986). These coherent accounts of self and the world are the structures individuals use to organize their experiences (Gergen 1992; McAdams 1988) and so are essential in understanding human actions (McAdams 1993; MacIntyre 1981; Sarbin 1986) and changes in self-identity. Narrative theory views social identities as plural, complex, changeable (Davis 1992; Fraser 1991) and interactively and discursively constructed within specific social contexts (Gergen and Gergen 1983; McAdams 1993).

Psychological abuse is an evolving process. Describing this process requires the use of narrative thinking to organize and sequence experience and to identify probable causes, uniting events, patterns, and themes. By using the narrative constructions of women who have been in psychologically abusive relationships, I was able to gain an understanding of the social processes and orders of events within these evolving relationships and to understand the evolving identities of the women.

My descriptive and phenomenological approach is based on the belief that individuals are the best and most reliable witnesses of their own experiences. So the narratives of the women participants were used to critique and expand existing information on psychological abuse. Like all individuals constructing life narratives, the women's narratives move from accounts of events to understanding why and how their lives developed as they did. As with all women, they created their lives under conditions they did not choose (Personal Narratives Group 1989). In their narratives, the intersection of the limitations of gender hierarchies and the social structure and the strength of individual agency can be seen.

Rather than attempting to fit the people to the theory, I listened for the theory or generalizations that guided the thoughts, feelings, and behavior of the women. My goal was to make their guiding generalizations visible (Denzin 1989b). The process involved reducing the collected information to its essential elements and then classifying, ordering, reassembling the phenomena and writing a realist narrative (Denzin 1989a) that depicts the experiences of the women. This new collective story that gives voice to women who have been marginalized or silenced can offer alternative knowledges for other women.

I believe this method of study can be done most compassionately and effectively when the researcher has a personal as well as professional understanding of the topic (Denzin 1989a). Therefore, it is important for you to understand my personal and professional viewpoint. I am a Caucasian American woman who grew up in a suburb of a large city as the oldest child and only daughter in a family with middle-class socioeconomic position and values. I was born at the end of the silent generation era, a few years before the beginning of the Baby Boomer generation. At that time, most middle-class women were programmed by traditional gender ideology. My family was somewhat atypical in relation to gender. My parents' expectations for and treatment of their sons and daughter were similar. Before her marriage and after her youngest child was in high school, my mother worked and had a successful career. She modeled the "superwoman" gender strategy, which is basically the pattern I have followed in my life. My father's mother owned a farm and ran a dairy business, so he grew up seeing women as capable. I have been married, had two children, gone through a difficult marriage and a long process of deciding to divorce, raised my children as a single parent, and counseled many women living in destructive relationships. For years I have been interested, both personally and professionally, in understanding the psychological destructiveness that characterizes so many marriages.

As a feminist studying the experience of women, I had two overarching goals. One was to contribute information that could be used to benefit women, and the other was to make participation in the study a positive and possibly empowering experience for the participants. I wanted to avoid the role of researcher as someone above and somehow better than the participants. Rather, I saw my role as the organizer of information provided by the participants.

QUESTIONS AND PARTICIPANTS

Two core questions gave focus to this project. First, how do women experience, explain, understand, respond to, and feel about being psychologically abused by their spouse? Second, what life experiences contributed to the turning points or epiphanies that ultimately led to the changes in their understandings and in their lives? This second question focused on those experiences that evoked critical reflection on their relationships and consideration of alternative possibilities. Presuming gender inequality, another overarching question was how the experiences of psychological abuse connect with popular culture beliefs about family and the relations between husbands and wives (Denzin 1991a). As with any phenomenon, in psychological abuse there is a constant interplay between thoughts, feelings, behavior, and constructed reality. To take into account this complexity, I looked at psychological abuse from an interpersonal, societal, intrapsychic, and process orientation.

To answer these questions, I collected biographies from sixteen women who identified that they were or are in psychologically abusive relationships. The participants were solicited from a number of sources, including practicing psychotherapists, a women's counseling center, church-sponsored divorce recovery groups, and a church-sponsored singles social group. Women were chosen who fit a definition of psychological abuse that was developed from work on psychological maltreatment of children (Brassard and Gelardo 1987; Hart and Brassard 1987; Nesbit and Karagianis 1987) and from studies of psychological abuse within physically abusive relationships (Ferraro 1979; Shepard 1991; Walker 1979). A psychologically abusive relationship was defined as a relationship involving verbal battering including repeated ridicule, verbal attacks, threats, accusation, verbal hostility, unrealistic expectations, domination, and/or name calling; economic deprivation involving withholding, regulating, and controlling money in coercive ways; social humiliation such as threatening or acting in embarrassing, aggressive, or obnoxious ways in order to force accommodation to demands; social isolation including determining allowable associates and establishing inappropriate restrictions; and sexual domination in terms of excessive demands for a sexual relationship and sexual put-downs.

In tape-recorded meetings, each woman told me about her life before the psychologically abusive marriage and explained how the relationship developed, how she experienced the psychological abuse, how she changed in response to the abusive relationship, and how her understanding of the relationship and herself changed over time. These interviews were joint projects formed by each of the women participants and me (Bruner 1990; Hyden 1994; Mishler 1986; Riessman 1990). In most cases, their narratives spilled out of them with few questions from me.

The women who willingly stayed active in the study from the beginning to the end read a summary of the findings and met in group meetings to review and critique the summary. They reported seeing it as an accurate reflection of their experience. Clinicians from a women's counseling center and psychotherapists who had worked with psychologically abused women also reviewed the summary and validated the accuracy of the descriptions, themes, and patterns.

PREVIOUS STUDIES OF PSYCHOLOGICAL ABUSE

The study of psychologically abusive relationships that are not also physically abusive is still exploratory (DeGregoria 1987; Follingstad, et al. 1990); however, awareness of psychological abuse in marriage as a serious and very damaging problem has been developing over recent years (Andersen, Boulette, and Schwartz 1991; Murphy and Casardi 1993; Tolman 1992; Walker 1984). Most previous studies of psychological abuse in marriage have considered it as a precursor to physical abuse or an aspect of physically abusive relationships, with psychological abuse seen as a correlated yet distinct phenomenon (Sonkin, Martin, and Walker 1985; Tolman 1989; Walker 1979); however, some research has been done on aspects of the psychological abuse of women as a unique form of interpersonal aggression (DeGregoria 1987; Hoffman 1984; Stets 1991).

A few studies have focused on the pervasiveness of psychological abuse or emotional abuse. In a 1985 study of divorced women, Cleek and Pearson found 55.5 percent identified emotional abuse as the cause of their divorce. In a 1989 study of psychological abuse in dating relationships of college women, Raymond and Bruschi found that 27 percent of the women studied had relationships characterized by high negative or abusive behavior and low positive or kind behavior. Of couples seeking services at a marital clinic, Straus (1979) reported 89 percent to 97 percent of married couples and more than two-thirds of engaged couples had engaged in all the psychological aggressive behaviors on the Conflict Tactics Scale during the previous twelve months. It is assumed that the actual number of women in emotionally abusive relationships is very high (Engels 1990).

Some authors have studied phenomena that either are similar to psychological abuse or include aspects of psychological abuse. Stets's (1991) study of dating relationships conceptualized psychological aggression as offensive and degrading verbal behavior that results in feelings of guilt, upset, or worthlessness. A general population survey showed a direct correlation between experiences of verbal aggression and probability of depression (Tolman 1992). Besides verbal aggression, there are other concepts that also include aspects of psychological abuse: nonphysical abuse (Hudson and McIntosh, 1981), indirect abuse (Gondolf 1987), emotional abuse (Nicarthy 1986), psychological coercion (Andersen 1985), and psychological maltreatment (Tolman 1989). Psychological coercion is defined as oppressive, degrading behavior that results in loss of ability to avoid further abuses and to be self-determining (Andersen, Boulette and Schwartz 1991). Tolman's psychological maltreatment scale, which was administered to 200 women at shelter intake, included fifty-eight items describing behaviors related to six themes: "attacking her personhood,... defining her reality,... controlling her contacts,... demanding subservience,... withholding positive reinforcers, ... threatening nonphysical punishment" (Tolman 1989, 163).

Hoffman (1984) studied psychological abuse using a definition that focused on the outcome of the abuse. She defined psychological abuse "as behavior sufficiently threatening to the woman so that she believes that her capacity to work, to interact in the family or society, or to enjoy good physical or mental health, has been or might be threatened" (37). Hoffman found that most of the men criticized the woman's area of strength. Being criticized in an area previously considered a strength is more painful than being criticized for something already accepted as a weakness. Although the women did not accept this devaluation at first, after constant repetition their self-concept changed. The women reported having no one with whom they could check out their perceptions. They were told and came to believe that this was the best relationship they could have. Some of the women had physical symptoms related to the ongoing mental stress of the relationship. Also, following being abusive to her, the men often demanded sex from her. The male physicians and psychologists the women had seen for their "nervous tension" and depression had not talked with them about their relationship problems. The women who left the relationships did so because they "could no longer endure the circumstances they were in" (40). The psychological well-being of their children was another important factor in leaving. Those who left the relationships reported an improvement in their emotional state, even though many of them were much more limited financially.

OVERVIEW

Our journey to understanding this complicated phenomenon will begin with chapter 1, "The Abuse of Women in Families," which summarizes existing information about physical and psychological abuse in marriage. The chapter "Life before Marriage" introduces each woman with a review of each one's life story up to the time of marriage. Chapters 3 and 5 describe the characteristics and the predominant interaction patterns seen in psychologically abusive relationships. The connections between the normative-oppressive, gender-polarized relationships of patriarchy and psychological abuse are discussed in chapter 4, "Because We Are Women."

Psychologically abusive relationships start out with the same high hopes that characterize other beginning relationships and often do not develop obvious problems until there is some competition for the wife's attention. Even after the problems start, years may pass before she is willing to name the difficulty and begin making changes. Chapters 6 through 9 focus on the process and mental and physical consequences of psychologically abusive relationships.

This book is directed to the many people who are trying to understand the experience of psychological abuse in marriage. This includes women in psychologically abusive marriages; practitioners working with these women; sociologists, social psychologists, psychologists, social workers, and other professionals who are concerned with the problems of women; and graduate students, our professionals of the future.

CAVEAT

Further study of the process in psychologically abusive relationships needs to be done. This research could include use of survey instruments so a broader sample of women could participate. Also, studies of the experiences of men who have been psychologically abused are needed. Often after problems are identified as issues for women, men claim "that happens to us, too." They are right; however, the frequency is often much less for men than for women. Although both men and women may be in psychologically abusive relationships, the quality of these relationships is affected by society's view of each gender. In patriarchical societies, men expect to be in the privileged positions, to have control and dominance at least over their wives and children. Women are expected to take care of men in exchange for security and protection from the violence in the world. Unfortunately, this dichotomy may lead to oppression, discriminatory practices, and domination. I believe psychological abuse of men is similar in some ways to psychological abuse of women but is different in many ways since patriarchal societies establish men as dominant.

1

THE ABUSE OF WOMEN IN FAMILIES

What would happen if one woman told the truth about her life?

—Muriel Rukeyer (1994, 217)

He did and said everything to keep me where he wanted me to be. He never acknowledged any of my accomplishments, not any I can recall. . . . When things seemed to be going pretty well, he'd figure out something else that I wasn't doing right and then he'd be on me every day about it. . . . See, the goalposts, I mean, every time I thought, this is working, they would be lifted up and moved down the field and I'd have to get all readjusted. (38-year-old public official)

When you would try to do something or talk to him, the comments that he would come back at you with just totally froze your insides. You couldn't even say anything. They just totally made you sick. (61-year-old administrative assistant)

Twenty years ago we began hearing women telling the truth about the physical abuse they were experiencing in their lives. Ten years ago we began hearing women telling the truth about the sexual abuse in their lives. Recently we began hearing women telling the truth about the psychological abuse in their lives. The stories are not new, only the voices and our ability to hear and understand. In the past, women were silent, believing that the problems in their relationships were their fault, thinking that they would be happy if only they tried harder to make their husbands happy, believing that the depression and anxiety they experienced meant that they were flawed. But consider how much depression, anxiety, and physical illness may be related to living with the ongoing pressure and pain of psychological abuse. This book describes psychologically abusive relationships, identifies the effects of these relationships on women, traces the process of these relationships, and offers effective methods for working with women who experience being trapped in psychologically abusive relationships.

Psychological abuse is the misuse of power by one person in order to create submission in the other person. This nonphysical form of abuse is characterized by exploitative or excessive expressions of power and dominance that demean, belittle, undermine, control, define, and criticize an individual in order to create submission (Hudson and McIntosh 1981; Murphy and Casardi 1993). Any nonphysical behavior that controls through the use of fear, humiliation, and verbal assault can be considered psychological abuse. In many marriages there are occasional abusive incidents or elements of the relationship that are abusive; however, to define a relationship as psychologically abusive there must be a continuous pattern of abuse.

In many cases, the emotional damage of psychological abuse is as serious as the consequences of physical abuse. In fact, some battered women identify the psychological abuse as worse (Ferraro 1979; Walker 1979, 1984). Because the erosion of self-esteem, self-confidence, and self-concept that results from psychological abuse is slow to heal (Nicarthy 1986; Walker 1979), psychic bruises are often deeper, more lasting, and more devastating than physical bruises.

Understanding psychological abuse is essential to continuing the process of developing healthy families. In order to become more effective facilitators of change, we need to broaden our understanding of psychologically abusive relationships. We need to look at this problem, identify its characteristics, bring it out in the open, and talk and write about it so women can better understand what is happening to them and begin to search for healthy alternatives.

THE FAMILY

A knowledge of "the operations of 'the family' is crucial in understanding the oppression of women" (Stanley and Wise 1983, 66). The family has been described as a domestic haven from the troubles of the world, but the idea of domestic haven ignores that men's dominance may be acted out in conflict, violence, and unequal distribution of family work. "Feminists have opened a whole new vista of inquiry by asking, *not what do women do for the family* (an older question), *but what does the family do for women? What does it do to women?*" (Bridenthal 1982, 235). Feminists identify that the family is a major site of women's oppression for two reasons. First, the financial structure of most families positions women as financially dependent on men. Second, within families the domestic and parenting work of women is often devalued, burdensome, and isolating (Barrett 1988; Thorne 1982).

Family as a social institution exists as an ideological construct. The meaning and definition of kinship, the structure of the household, and the ideology of family have varied a great deal in different types of societies. Our current concept of nuclear family is "an achievement of industriousness, respectability and regulation" (Barrett 1988, 203), not a pregiven or natural, universal entity. The family provides the ideological center for a variety of themes related to gender and sexuality, including feminine nurturance, romantic love, self-sacrifice, maternalism, masculine protection, and financial support. Definitions of appropriate gender and family behavior are socially created and are transmitted by the media. Historically, television shows have produced idealized images of the family as a well-functioning group, usually organized around traditional gender roles, that offers its members nurturance and structure. For women, the family is offered as a solution to their dissatisfactions (Turner and Shapiro 1986).

In reality, families struggle to replicate the ideology of the family (Barrett 1988). Children often internalize and enact stereotyped images provided by the media (Stanley and Wise 1983). For example, years ago I overheard my young son explain to a friend that his father had an office downtown (in fact it was my office) and that I stayed home and cleaned house (actually I worked full-time and had the house cleaned). Apparently the television image was more real or more acceptable in his mind than was his experience. This dichotomy between the family as a structural institution, an ideological construct, and the family of lived experience often exists (Stanley and Wise 1983).

The ideology of the family as a place of nurturance is not the lived experience of many women and children. For many women, the family is a place of unending work, abuse, and domination. Gallop (1985) identifies that the family is and always has been the "privileged locus of the exploitation of women" (79). Although marriage has a protective effect on men, it has been found to be "detrimental for women in terms of both mental and physical health" (Hare-Mustin 1991, 65).

For many people, deBeauvoir's 1961 book *The Second Sex* opened the discussion of the problems of women in families. Betty Friedan's *The Feminine Mystique* (1963), which described "the problem that has no name," popularized understanding of the degradation, isolation, and discontent of housewives that has since been explored by many authors (e.g., Ehrenreich and English 1978; Goodrich, et al. 1988; Swerdow 1978). The positions of wife and mother have low social value and limited autonomy and can involve constraining, repressive, routinized service. Maintaining these roles often has a debilitating effect on women (Kravetz 1986, 109). I remember a period when I was not working and was living in a new neighborhood with my husband and our outgoing, young daughter, Amy. In that neighborhood, I was "Amy's Mom." I loved being Amy's mother, but going from being known as an individual and a professional to being identified by a role and a relationship felt diminishing to me.

PHYSICAL ABUSE OF WOMEN IN THE FAMILY

Since 1971, considerable research and clinical interest have focused on physical abuse of women in the family; however, before that time physical abuse had been ignored (Gelles 1976; O'Brien

1981). In 1971, Erin Pizzey founded Chiswick Women's Aid in England. This was a place where women and children could discuss their concerns. "The overwhelming majority who came were battered women" (Gelb 1983, 250). From these experiences, Pizzey wrote *Scream Quietly or the Neighbors Will Hear* (1974). That book led to the creation of the British Women's Aid Federation.

The first battered-women's shelter in the United States was established in St. Paul, Minnesota, in 1974. By the late 1970s, there were 250 shelters across the United States, and domestic violence was viewed by many people as a social problem and a public issue requiring governmental legislative intervention (Gelb 1983). The founders of these battered-women's shelters conceived of a different way and decided that women should not have to endure violent relationships.

The irony in our society is that the family is symbolized as a place of affection and nurturance, but it is the place where violence is most tolerated (Collier, Rosaldo, and Yanagisako 1982). The family is our society's most violent social institution (Gelles and Cornell 1990). The shocking thing about wife abuse is not just the amount of abuse but that women are being hurt by someone they love and believe loves them. The impact of the injury is intensified by the emotional pain and the violation of trust of being hurt by someone you love (Ferraro 1979).

Many families are not nurturing or even safe for women and children. "One in four wives is beaten by her husband, and cases of incest, 97% of which are perpetrated by men, are estimated at 400,000 per year" (Kosof 1985). Using a definition of physical abuse that included all types of physical violence, Straus (1977) concluded that at least half of the women in the United States would experience some type of physical abuse during their marriage. These figures do not consider the damage done to women and children by oppression, domination, and psychological abuse.

Both physical and psychological abuse can be explained as an extension of the patriarchical pattern of gender polarity that establishes dominance and control as central aspects of the masculine and as inappropriate in the feminine (Davis 1991; Smith 1990). For some men, the need for power and authority is satisfied in the world of work; for others, this need is acted out in the family leading to tensions which are sometimes expressed in violence (McGrath 1979) or psychological abuse. Research has shown that this patriarchal mandate is directly related to wife-beating (Dobash and Dobash 1979; Ferree 1990; Kurz 1989; Hanmer and Maynard 1987; Schechter 1982; Schechter and Gary 1988; Schwendinger and Schwendinger 1983; Straus, Gelles, and Steinmetz 1980; Yllö 1993; Yllö and Straus 1984).

Nonphysical (or psychological) abuse in marriage is another aspect of the broader system of male dominance. Psychological abuse involves oppression and exists within a society structured by inequality, driven by the need to control and dominate, and characterized by power dichotomies. Psychological abuse involves abuse of interpersonal power. Interpersonal power is the ability of one person to impose his or her will on another person (Laird 1991a). When one person possesses resources (shelter, financial or emotional support, etc.) needed by the other, he is in a position of control and power. "Power is force or interpersonal dominance actualized in human relationships through manipulation and control" (Denzin 1989a, 29). Power acts to limit, contain, disqualify, and deny. In families, male abuse of interpersonal power subordinates women and promotes dependency. In this powerless situation, women can easily become victims of psychological abuse.

WOMEN'S STORIES

This book is about the strengths, the struggles, and the pains of women. Their stories must be told to break the patterns of isolation that have left individual women believing their situations were unique and would not be understood by others. Although the women's first names have been changed and all identifying information excluded, their narratives are vividly real and will surely speak to any person who has ever felt abused. It is their stories that need to be told and understood, their stories that can break the isolation of individual women, their stories that shed light on the phenomenon of psychological abuse of women in families, their stories that expand and enrich other women's possibilities for self-construction. I acted as the collector of the stories, the identifier of the common themes, the connector

of theory to experience, the organizer of the wealth of information, and the writer. My goal has been to let their stories create
the understanding and illuminate the theories that governed
their lives.

Do the themes, descriptions, and processes in these narratives
have universal significance that can help us understand psychological abuse and develop appropriate therapeutic interventions
and approaches? The participants and those who have read this
material think these unique experiences are instances of universal
themes. As reader, you will also evaluate whether these women's
truths reflect a more universal truth "around which the particular experiences of particular women vary" (Young 1990b, 17).

Although I doubt if any of the women I interviewed had read
Sartre (1981), like Sartre they understood that they were simul-
taneously unique individuals with diverse backgrounds and experiences and strikingly similar instances of a more universal
experience. They agreed that the themes, descriptions, and processes applied to all of them. One woman recommended that I
should state how "alike all of us are." She said,

I think that would be a really important thing for people to know. When
you started you had some things in mind that you figured you'd see,
but then, all of a sudden, you listened to the stories and, oh my gosh,
basically we're all living in different walls, but we're all the same. That's
important for them to know. That's universal, that takes it from us being
a unique group of this happened to you, oh, darn, to oh my gosh, this
must be universal.

Another woman echoed that theme, saying, "I just realized,
after reading the summary, how similar everybody is. When I
was reading, I was thinking, 'Oh yeah, he did that to me, too.'
It's not the things he did, it is the attitude about him. It seems
like it is so common. I thought my husband was the only one
like that." Summarizing, a third woman said, "I'm sitting here
taking all of this in, all the feelings and all the emotions. Although our situations are different, everything just seems the
same."

In the following chapters, the narratives of these women will
be used to confirm, expand, and add depth to what has previ-

ously been learned about psychologically abusive relationships. In the next chapter, each woman will be introduced through her story of her life before her marriage. As you hear about this diverse group, you may come to believe as I do that women from all backgrounds are vulnerable to psychological abuse.

2

LIFE BEFORE MARRIAGE

Have you ever felt like nobody?
Just a tiny speck of air.
When everyone's around you,
And you are just not there.

—Karen Crawford, age 9

I wish I could include a picture of the women who shared their life narratives with me. You would see such an interesting, diverse group ranging in age from 24 to 63, including three racial groups and most socioeconomic levels. All the women completed high school, three completed two years of college, five are college graduates, and one has a master's degree. In my view each woman is attractive, but many have lost the ability to see their beauty. From a picture you might guess that several women are professionals, but you would not see the pain that they have experienced, because they tend to hide their pain from other people and sometimes even from themselves.

In this chapter, each woman will be introduced as she relates her narrative up to the time of entering the psychologically abusive relationship; the stories of their experiences as psychologically abused wives will be included in chapters 4 through 10. As I heard about their inner lives and about their lived experiences, I realized again and again that attention must be paid to their silent cries, that their voices need to be heard, and that their stories can inform others. With the exception of some summary comments and the editorial shifts necessary to go from spoken narratives to written stories, I have used their voices to tell the story.

TAMIKA

Tamika grew up in the South. Although her parents were very poor, she described her childhood as happy. She lived with her parents and younger siblings.

What I saw was my mother and father able to cooperate. They were sharecroppers and so they worked together. . . . There was arguments, but it didn't seem to create a real concern to me. . . . During the peak season of farming, . . . they took us to the field with them. There was times, when I was young, that my mother and father left us at the house, left me in charge; but it didn't feel real strenuous.

After her parents separated, Tamika lost contact with her father. She and her family moved to her maternal grandfather's house where her great-grandmother and uncle lived.

That was the first time that I came in contact with a very rigid kind of role in a male. My grandfather was very rigid, he was very distant. He saw his role as he put food in the house and made sure everybody got what they needed in terms of food, clothes, and shelter and that was it.

Her mother remarried when Tamika was eight.

My stepfather was an A-1 abuser, A-1! This man was one physical, verbal, whatever. . . . He was really an abusive human being. I fought this man, for the survival of myself and my sisters. . . . The man didn't like us. . . . Anytime my young brother would cry, he [stepfather] would get upset and blame someone and sometimes he would just chase us. I would even take my brother and my sisters and I would go hide under the house until my mother came home. . . . I felt real responsible for my siblings.
When mama came out of that marriage, she attracted another situation. She started to date this guy and he was abusive. When he came into the house, I say "You get out." I had a poker and I was going to

show the man. I'm sure I was. When I think about it, I was going to hurt this man.

If you are wondering where this young girl learned strength, listen to what she told me about her great-grandmother.

My great-grandmother lived with us. By now she had lost all of her sight, and so she lived with us. . . . I was asked just recently, who was the one person that most impacted my life. If I had to look back, it would be my great-grandmother 'cause she was the most stable. She was the most strength, she was wise, she was the history. . . . Even now when I see myself reflecting and dealing with my life, it's like my great-grandmother. She gave my life stability, a kind of pride and history.

She maintained the culture. She told the stories. She was really an interesting woman. . . . Her daughter went to college, and she had a son; he went to college. My great-grandmother was the first born out of slavery, but she was a very intelligent woman and she wanted her kids to go to school. When we would come home, we had to sit at her knee and talk about what we learned in school.

Talking about why she married her first husband, Tamika said,

I was about seventeen when I noticed that my mother wanted power over the house. That's the only thing that I can give it. I was more or less sickly. I don't know if I psychologically did this or not, but I hated the field. And they would say, "Well she doesn't do well in the field so leave her home to take care of the house."

So I took care of the house, made the dinner, and all the other good stuff. It didn't matter to me. It didn't hurt me any that I didn't get to go to the field.

I started to date when I was about sixteen. . . . My mother didn't like him. She didn't want us to date. I was too young and she didn't want him around me, so he went away. He said, "I'm coming back to get you when you're old enough to marry me."

He would write and sometime I'd get his letters and then eventually my mother started to destroy the letters. . . . One day I went home and I found one in the trash with a picture and the letter was torn up. He was saying in that letter that he was coming home on leave. My mother had put the word out that he had better not show his face at our house. So I never did get to really date the guy or anything.

My mother come up with this idea that I was kind of sexually active. . . . My mother would say nasty, I mean nasty, like, "You're going to go out and get pregnant, you're just being a bitch." And I'm going like, who is this woman, who is this human being? And my great-grandmother had heard her. My great-grandmother called me one day, and she said, "Well, what in the world has got into your mother?" And I said, "I have no idea."

Tamika described a time when her mother hit her with a board.

This is the first time I can remember this woman really hurting me. I mean she just took a board and started hitting me in my side, just hitting me in my side. And I felt like, I don't know, it was just terror. I said, "Mom, what is wrong with you? Why are you doing this?" I'm looking at this woman and saying, who is she? . . . This was like the high point, 'cause she had been verbally abusive and all of a sudden this physical abuse.

After being hit, Tamika decided to get married to escape from her mother. She had been dating a man she described as charming and charismatic. He lived in the city and had a car, which impressed Tamika's mother.

I programmed him to talk to my mother about marrying me, right? And so he came one Sunday evening and he sat down and my mother said, "I didn't know you was thinkin' about getting married." It was like real shock time, you know. "Are you sure that you want to do that?" And I said, "Yep, I'm sure I want to do it, mother."

So I go through this whole charade. My mother wanted him to know she was in charge. The one thing that the womans pride themselves on is a wonderful daughter who had not gotten pregnant. Oh, it was a wedding. We had a reception on the lawn and flowers and church and everything, a powerful wedding. For me it was an escape. And I know that. I know that now more than I knew that then.

As Tamika describes herself within her early life story, she uses words like in charge, capable, strong, and intelligent like her great-grandmother. She saw herself as able to defend herself against or get away from physical abuse. Throughout her life story, these self-images continued to affect decisions she made about herself and her relationships. When this study began Tamika was in her early fifties, a striking, vivid, energetic woman who runs her own business. Tamika has moved through several relationships in her life with each relationship experienced as more satisfying than the previous one.

KATHY

Kathy described her childhood through college as being positive, with few difficulties. As an only child who grew up in a small town, "I was just raised in a very traditional manner. My parents got along. Everything was great in my childhood."

Kathy went away to a private high school. She was shy and felt miserable being away from the familiar, but by college she had a great time. She met her husband during her freshman year.

It was my first real serious relationship, real serious. We just continued seeing each other. It was just sort of understood we would get married and we did.

We had a gorgeous, big wedding. He had just finished his first year of [graduate] school and I did my master's in a year so we would be ready to go out into the work force at the same time. I finished my undergraduate work before we got married and then I did my graduate work the first year I was married.

Kathy was raised to be a traditional wife and mother, to live the middle-class American dream. She has two children and a professional career which she returned to after the children were both in school. Kathy looks like television's version of a suburban housewife and mom. Her appearance hides the years of pain she experienced living with a deceitful, demanding alcoholic. Like many of the other women, trying to maintain her family was so important to Kathy that she was willing to stay in an unhappy marriage for seventeen years. When I met Kathy, she was in her late thirties and had been separated from her husband for six months. They were in the process of working out the divorce settlement.

DOROTHY

Dorothy is the second child in a family of three children. She had all the nice material things: "my own pink room, dolls, stable, pool, private school education." She said, "We went to church every Sunday."

I remember having anything monetary that any child could ever want, but being terribly neglected emotionally. My father was very successful at what he did. He worked really hard. I would say he was a workaholic. My mom was a housewife who was more interested in what her agenda was instead of being a nurturing kind of person. I feel like I was a kind of a lonely child who really needed a lot more attention than I ever got. I was good in school and even that wasn't recognized. I would bring home my report card, and it was just kind of a given that Dorothy would do well.

But there was more than the pain of being ignored.

I was abused sexually by my uncle. He would give me old silver dollars after and he would tell me not to spend them because they were old and worth more than a $1.00. I would wonder why he only gave them to me and not my sisters and I hid them in my room just like I hide what he said and did to me. I became a loner, went to school, came home, stayed by myself. This lasted for years.

At about thirteen years old, I realized this isolation was not normal. When I started high school, I joined clubs and got in sports. I had some friends.

But just as Dorothy was beginning to find her place in the world, her family moved. She had trouble breaking into the established social groups at her new high school, but did meet her husband there.

We went out a few times and got along well. He wanted to spend time with me and take me places. He had a job, but every free minute I spent with him. . . . I finally gave in to be more serious with him. After that, we had a regular sexual relationship.

Dorothy got pregnant. She graduated from high school early, got married, and had her first child all in the same year.

In discussing her childhood, Dorothy uses words such as neglected, not recognized, or supported. She describes herself as lonely but able to persevere through crisis. These themes continued in her marriage until she began to find her own source of strength. Today she presents herself as a competent, capable professional who put herself through school and established herself as a professional in her community. In her late thirties, Dorothy has two children. She was married for almost twenty years before separating.

CAROL

Carol identified her childhood as "lost, lonely, and confused. I grew up in a very dysfunctional family." She said that her father was an alcoholic and both her parents physically abused her. "My dad has a very terrible temper. . . . He was very controlling, very violent." Carol has one older brother and four younger siblings.

My dad just stayed out really late. My mom would usually go to work after we got home from school. As a waitress she worked in the evenings. I would be responsible for finishing up the dinner, making sure that the dishes got done and everything got cleaned up and everybody did their homework; and then when my dad came home, his dinner got warmed up, whatever time that was. Usually I would wait up for my mother, even on school nights. I was her emotional support. She would tell me all about their problems and things she was trying to deal with herself.

As a kid I just took what I was dealt and handled it. I never really complained. My mom has told me that I was a perfect child. I was real responsible; I could do anything. I was an adult. I wasn't a child.

My parents are both very controlling. They want to know everything about your life and if they don't, then they are very critical of you.

They think that they were very good parents. And we didn't do without. We had food, clothing, and shelter; but I remember being willing to give that up if I could just get somebody to care about me and to love me instead of criticizing me or beating me.

Carol lives near her parents and describes her parents' way of treating her as unchanged. She still waits on them and takes care of them when she visits in their home.

I want it to be so different and it's not any different. It's never going to be any different and that's hard to accept 'cause all my life I have tried to make it different. I tried to fix their relationship. I can remember, even at eight and ten years old, I would fix anniversary dinners for them. I thought maybe they would have a dinner together and that we'd be a family, but it never worked. It just never worked.

I think I have more problems dealing with my issues with my mother because she was there most of the time, and she was physically abusive and emotionally abusive. . . . I think the reason I don't have as many issues with my dad is because he just wasn't there. I was angry with him for not being there, but somehow, when he was there he was tired, drunk, and beating us. So I was just as happy for him not to be there. And now, I can't carry on a conversation with my father 'cause I don't know what to say to him. I don't know how to talk to him. He's just like my mother in that he never lets you forget something. He's very critical of my divorce. He's very critical of my attorney. My dad always knew everything. Whatever my dad thought of something, it was the right way, the right thought, the right way to handle things. Nobody could ever do it right for him.

Carol talked about what attracted her to her ex-husband.

I wanted to marry him. . . . It's real amazing because the things I liked most in him then were the things that I hated when I left him.

His family is very dysfunctional. There is a lot of chaos in his family too and there was alcoholism. His father drank a lot. . . . His dad didn't really beat them. He mostly tore up the house when he was drinking. There was so much chaos in our families.

[Her ex-husband] could hold everything together. It didn't bother him. He was strong. He had no emotional feelings whatsoever about what was going on in the family, and I was just falling apart at the seams. I wanted so badly to have what he had and be able to ignore all that and not to let it bother me. I thought that I would gain that.

When I met him, I was just real impressed. He excelled in school. He excelled at work. I've worked with him and he can do just anything. Anything that is put before him, he can handle it, and I wanted that too.

We started dating and we talked about getting married when I got out of school and then I ended up pregnant. We decided we would go ahead and get married and then I would just finish up the credits that I needed.

What's interesting is that I married a person just like my father, extremely unemotional. The only emotion that my father knew was anger and that's the only emotion that [her ex-husband] knows. He has no emotions whatsoever. He never smiles. He hardly speaks to you. You just don't know how he feels about anything until he gets angry.

As a child, Carol saw herself as lost, lonely, confused, and dominated, but also as a responsible caretaker who tried to please others. These qualities continued to be central until the ending stages of her marriage. Although she didn't work during her marriage, she now has a job working with young children. When I met Carol, she was in her late thirties. A mother of two children, Carol was married for almost twenty years before separating.

TAMMI

Tammi's childhood was characterized by abuse and violence. Her young parents lived in a rural area and were very poor. Neither had much education. Her father had a serious drinking problem. When drunk, he beat up her mother.

They were very country people, mountain people, and very hindered in many ways. Like my dad, he just maybe went to fifth grade. He was a coal miner. My mom was being physically abused while she was pregnant with me. I figure that's why she hated me all along.

She was jealous of me all her life. Because my dad, he used to call me "Daddy's little girl." She was jealous of his feelings toward me. . . . She was an abusive woman: emotionally, verbally, physically. She didn't like me at all. . . . I always feared her and I never wanted to be around her. I never knew what she was going to say to me or what she was going to do.

Most of the time he [her dad] tried to be good to me. . . . He wasn't abusive toward me verbally or physically or anything like that. He was more neglectful than anything just because he was alcoholic. He would stay gone, drunk. He was incapable of showing the affection that was necessary, but he would want to take me with him . . . to some of the little bars. . . . They put money in the jukebox and I'd dance on the tables and people would laugh and give me potato chips and Cokes and I would just be happy.

When Tammi was quite young, her mother became an alcoholic and often left her children. Tammi was a neglected child who had to take on adult responsibilities at a very young age. "My mother slept with a lot of men during her alcoholic years. She was always having somebody around. It was just so crazy."

During those years, Tammi and her brother experienced a great deal of violence between her parents. Both parents were in and out of jail and often gone. The children were sometimes sent to live with relatives. Tammi described herself as

a very quiet, good girl . . . until I was nine or ten. At that time I changed. I became very rebellious and angry and hateful and started cutting school, stealing things. When they would catch me stealing, I wouldn't talk to them or even tell them who I was. . . . I was put in the juvenile center when I was ten, when they caught me cutting school and stealing.

By the time she was twelve, Tammi was sexually abused by a relative and ran away from home.

When I got back home, they beat up on me. My mom especially because of my taking off. She called me her usual—slut and whore—that was her favorite names for me. She hardly ever wanted to say anything good. She just cussed and hit at me and called me names. I was used to that. I expected that's what I would get when I got home. And from then on, I was a habitual runaway.

I really got crazy. I started running around with boys in cars at the age of eleven and twelve. . . . I was even playing strip poker by the age of eleven with the boys. I was very much a tomboy and in a lot of fights in school. . . . I kept on being very much a loner. They [other kids] wouldn't leave me alone, you know, and they would push me and push me and push me until I would turn on them. Then when I did, I was so full of anger that I would hurt them very bad. I wouldn't quit beating on 'em once I got them down. So I got in trouble a few times. I got expelled from school for fighting, although they were very perplexed by me 'cause I made straight As. But at the same time, I was always in a lot of trouble. So I was very intelligent, but I was in a lot of trouble.

At fourteen, I got pregnant and ran away. That was a major turning point. It got me out of my alcoholic home.

Although she was frequently returned home by the authorities, her pattern of running away continued during her adolescence.

After the father of Tammi's child was sent to prison for robbery, Tammi went to live with his brother who physically abused her. Talking about this period, Tammi said:

I would drink a lot, sometimes til I would throw up. I didn't know why. I know why now. I was in such pain, you know, and my anger, it was to help control some of the rage I felt. I got better when I drank and happier and I laughed a lot.

When Tammi was eighteen, she was violently raped and beaten. From that time on, she said that she "was full of fear of men." As a young adult, Tammi married a man she described as a "hippie." He introduced her to drugs.

Within six months after being married, I was gone. I just left. I had an eating disorder there about that time. I would hide and eat food and I would fast for a week and I would throw up. . . . But I didn't know why I was doing those things at the time—the drugs, the eating disorders, the sexual addiction. At the time, I didn't even see it as a sexual addiction. I just thought I'm doing what men do. Men have sex all the time with people and why can't I? This was my thinking, you know. It was late sixties, early seventies. . . . Everybody was doing drugs and having sex. It wasn't any big thing.

Tammi's childhood memories of happy times dancing on the bar continued into adulthood when she saw being a dancer in bars as a way to be in control in relation to men. For many years, Tammi worked in bars as a dancer and as a bartender.

I learned how to manipulate and control men in that environment because you have all the control in there, the woman does. The men have no control at all. You say what goes and that's all there is to it. If they get out of line, you get the bouncer, you know, and they know that's what they have to deal with. They're going to get punched out by this big guy at the door, so they have to jump to your tune.

As a dancer, I was very much in control of men and manipulating them to get money from them and to make my living; but at the same time, I was so messed up inside and I had not a clue of it. I thought I was doing fine. I thought, well, I've got a job and I'm sending my daughter to dance classes and she has nice clothes and I'm making good money and I have a better car. . . . But along in there somewhere, I got a little bit crazy and I can't hardly remember it all, up to the time when my dad died, 'cause I took a different turn.

Before my dad died, . . . I had a spiritual experience where I quit the drugs and everything, you know. . . . From that time on, I changed. . . . I was raised atheist. I was taught not to believe in God. I had no hope, no belief at all. My mother was totally opposed to it. She would not let me go to church. She did find out one time that I was going to Sunday school and she punished me for it. So I had a fear. I couldn't go to church or I'd get a whipping. She said, "There's no such thing as God. That's a fairy tale. That's a stupid story."

I had no faith in God. So many things had happened to me I thought there can't be no God or He would have helped me. I didn't realize He did help me. He let me survive that rape when I should have been dead. And when my mom tried to kill me. There's many times I should have been dead that people tried to kill me. I'm lucky to be alive.

Tammi felt the spiritual experience she had was a major turning point in her life.

I started bartending at night and going to beauty school during the day. I decided, after my spiritual experience, I wanted to get out of bars. . . . I started feeling different about myself. I started feeling better about myself. I was more confident with less drug use. I wasn't as angry. It was getting harder to provoke me.

I dated men, but I was always in control of what was going on. . . . I'd become, after so many years, a master of manipulation of men and controlling of men to get what I wanted from them because I knew how to do it. I knew their weak points. I'm a very intelligent woman, and I became like them. I was one of them—emotionally unavailable, manipulative, controlling. . . . I did not want another man to be able to hurt me in any way. They had already done enough and I was fed up. It was my way of figuring out a way to protect myself and still be involved with men to a certain extent because, at the time, I was definitely a sex addict. I had a problem with it. The sex was a big coverup in my emotions, like a lot of men do.

Tammi has been in two psychologically abusive relationships. She decided she wanted to be in "a real relationship" and "fell madly in love" with a man who was an alcoholic. His alcoholism led to Tammi going to an Alcoholics Anonymous meeting and then to an Al-Anon meeting. Since then, she has pursued "recovery: one-on-one counseling, group therapy, ACOA, Al-Anon." But her next relationship was with an "emotionally unavailable man" who was also alcoholic. Tammi was just ending this relationship when I met her.

As Tammi relates her childhood and early adult story, she describes herself as able to escape from physically abusive situations, as a fighter, an intelligent person who knows how to be "like a man." Tammi is a bright, positive, attractive, young-looking forty-year-old woman who has an adult daughter. Her story, like Tamika's, is one in which her relationships with men have gradually gotten less abusive, from a teenage relationship with a man who physically and psychologically abused her to her most recent relationship, which was psychologically abusive.

BECKY

Becky was raised by her mother. She always longed for her father's attention, but he was rarely home and not interested in his children.

My dad was a truck driver and so he was gone all the time. My mother practically raised us. When he did come home, it was preferential treatment for him. He always said, "I am the king and this is my castle and the king runs the castle and this is the way it's going to be" and rules, rules, rules. I don't ever remember him ever touching me, except to spank me, except the day I got married.

He would come home from his runs on the road and we would want to climb on his lap and see him. He would say, "Get these kids away from me, I'm tired. I just want to sit here and have a beer and eat something and go to bed." And that was how it was every time. I don't ever remember it any different than that.

I remember my mom leaving him. I remember he hit her once and she left him. She said, "I will not tolerate him doing that to me," so he never did anything to my Mom. He was loving to her, but he wasn't to us. I don't know why.

Becky tried very hard to please her father, but nothing she could do was good enough.

I would come home with 5 As and a B+ and he would say, "What is this B? What is this? What happened?" He was teasing us. He did it to all of us, and we didn't know that. We had no idea he was teasing us. And he did stuff like that all the time and that just crushed me. Nothing I ever did was ever good enough.

As a child, I was terrified of my father and not very happy. I was extremely shy, making it very hard to make friends. I remember hating school because of my shyness. I vividly remember how my best friend abandoned me on the first day of school in the first grade. This was to be a lifelong pattern with what people refer to as friends.

When I was about thirteen or fourteen, I remember wading up and down in a mud puddle in front of our house. There was a guy that was a friend of mine right across the street; we'd just gone to get ice cream cones together. We were just laughing, having a good time, and my dad came out there and he said, "Why don't you two grow up." Just everything to put me down, everything.

He never trusted me and I never did anything to violate his trust. My older brother got in trouble all the time so I was just like, wow. And I didn't do anything, I didn't stay out late, I didn't drink, I didn't do anything; but I always was put down.

My mom told me the other day, he always thought I would end up pregnant. I said, "I can't believe that." I never had sex in high school, nothing, nothing. You know, be a good girl for your Dad. He'd always sit there and say "Well, good girls don't do this and they don't do this." You know, a list of rules again. And I had to follow this list of rules.

I liked to read books. I remember I would go to the library and get lots of books. Well, when I was about eight or nine years old, he came home one day and he jumped on me because why wasn't I helping my mom do this and do that in the house? So from then on, I was expected to do everything and pretty soon I was doing everything. I washed and waxed their cars when I was older. I mean I did everything for these people. In fact, I was the last one out of the house. But I couldn't please him.

None of the boyfriends was ever any good. This one guy I dated, I knew he was running around on me, but I wanted him. My Dad came home and called me a dumb ass and that just really hurt a lot. I thought, "How can you do that to your children?" It wasn't that I was doing anything, but just because he thought that I was stupid for putting up with it. . . . I felt always judged, always on the line to be judged and I didn't see why. I still don't know why.

Becky's mother taught her to put everyone else first.

You know, I've never been able to have anything. . . . My mother didn't even realize it, but different things I wanted for Christmas when I was a kid, like I wanted this Barbie Doll case, . . . she gave it to my sister; and a movie projector thing, she bought it, but she gave it to my brother. She doesn't even know she did that.

She's a sweetheart, but she has ruined me because she taught me to take care of everybody else first and not me. Of course, my dad did too, you know, "You help your mother do everything."

Becky talked about many times when no matter what she did her father was critical of her.

I just couldn't please him no matter what I did. I tried with the straight As, I tried everything and nothing pleased him. I couldn't do anything right.

I wasn't a problem child, I never got in trouble, I never did anything. I never violated curfew. I just couldn't please him, nothing would work.

Both of Becky's parents were insensitive to her needs. They smoked even though she was allergic to smoke; it made her "about half sick." Looking back, Becky thinks that her ex-husband is a lot like her father.

My husband is just like that, very demanding. I remember my mom, my dad would want steak. He would come home from a long run, so she would go and buy him steak and we had to eat hamburger. That was something that always bothered me.

Becky met her husband when she was in her early twenties; he was a lot older. She began dating him when he was going through his divorce. Talking about their long courtship, Becky explained how he charmed her.

He listened to all the right kind of music, the right kind of restaurants, nothing like these other guys had ever taken me to, nice restaurants, nice things. I just couldn't believe this, it was wonderful. Nobody was ever nice to me like this ever before. He was gentle and caring and giving, very loving to his children. And I just fell hook, line, and sinker, the whole bit. He did everything for me and he was nice. My parents thought he was wonderful.

I knew he had screwed around with this other woman behind his first wife's back. I knew that and he was still seeing her while he saw me. I knew that, but I thought, idiot here, well he said, "No, I love you."

He would call, all these nice phone calls, flowers, cards, everything just kept coming and coming and the only thing that was weird during the whole relationship was his daughter. . . . He wanted this child constantly with him.

I didn't realize that he had been seeing this woman all through, before, during, and after our marriage, every bit of it, and so the courtship was great. I thought he loved me. He bought me this huge diamond ring. Who would spend that kind of money if they didn't love somebody and care? But to him money is nothing; it is, but it isn't, you know. But he didn't ever abuse me in any way in talking or anything at all before.

In her childhood, Becky learned that "men are king," that they teased, criticized, judged, dominated, and couldn't be pleased. These beliefs were confirmed in her marriage. Now, Becky is in her late thirties and has one child. She has lived in small towns all her life, but recently moved to a city to get away from her husband. They were married for eleven years and had been separated for two months when I first met Becky.

DEBBI

Debbi's mother was the classic traditional woman, so that was what Debbi learned.

I was brought up to take care of men. My mother didn't work. My mother took care of the house, took care of what had to be taken care of. You get dinner on the table at a certain time, breakfast has to be at a certain time, do clothes, and that's what she did. She didn't have a life of her own, at all. She didn't have friends, she didn't go anywhere, she didn't do anything, she didn't drive. It was sad. It was real sad. She lived her life through my father and through me, and I hated that. I disliked her for that, for letting her life get like that. . . . I just started thinking about it and that was one of the things I was angry about is that my mother never had a life of her own and always made me feel that I had to share everything with her, my life with her, my friends with her.

Debbi is an attractive woman who is easy to be with and interesting to talk with; but in our society where women are taught that physical perfection is necessary in order to be chosen, Debbi feared that no man would want her.

I was never worthy of anybody to want me. I don't know whether I ever brought this up, but I have a physical handicap that made me feel that a man would never want me. I was born with a [minor physical difference]. I went through all my growing up years, the teenage years, you know, thinking I was different. And when I began to date, I was so self-conscious. . . . I met a fellow out of high school, it may have been my senior year. And we dated and, you know, things happened, and we started going together and we were going to get married. It was just like I would have taken anybody, not to be without somebody.

After high school, Debbi went to work, and the fellow she was dating joined the service. Eventually he ended the relationship. She said that "every guy that I went with, there were one, two, three, four, they all broke up with me. I never broke up with any of them." By the time Debbi met her ex-husband she was feeling desperate. Their relationship was off and on for awhile, but eventually he decided to marry her.

I'd always been self-conscious about my [physical difference], and he said, "I'd like for you to have an operation to correct it." I really was hesitant. I really didn't want to, but he said, "I really want you to have it." I thought, "Well, if he wants to do this, if he wants this."

There I began doing what he wanted. If it was up to me, I would have never had it done, but I went ahead and he paid for it. He laughed and he said, "That was my engagement ring." So I had that done and he came out and we got married.

It [the physical difference] had never seemed to bother him through our whole marriage. I look back and I think, I guess that probably played a big part in why I let everything happen to me that happened to me. Let him verbally abuse me, mistreat me. It's because I really didn't think I would ever be desirable to a man.

As a girl, Debbi was self-conscious. She saw herself as unattractive and thought that no man would want her. In her marriage, she accepted a traditional role and tried to keep her husband happy. After being married nineteen years, her husband divorced her a few months before I met her. Debbi is in her midforties, has four children, and had been a full-time housewife and mother until the time of the divorce. After the divorce, she went back to the professional career she began after college.

AMY

Speaking about her childhood, Amy begins by focusing on the positives: "I had a normal, happy childhood. . . . I have a younger sister. We are very close. My father was a good father. He used to play with us and do things with us." When she talks about the pain in her life, she tends to quickly move on to something positive.

My parents were divorced when I was ten, but I never heard them fighting. They just didn't talk to each other. I guess they just drifted apart. My father left. . . . I guess I was angry when he left us, but I didn't stay angry long.

My mother remarried when I was eleven. He is a wonderful man, the best thing that ever happened to my sister and me. . . . When I was thirteen, my father and his new wife moved to Oregon. I haven't seen him since. . . . I didn't invite him to my wedding. . . . I just lost touch with him.

Amy began dating her husband when she was in high school. He was older and had a child. In contemplating the beginning of their relationship, she said, "I was having problems with my mother and he supported me against my mother. . . . Marrying him was a way to get out of the house."

Amy is a beautiful young woman who looks like a model but is a full-time student and mother of a young child. The pattern she learned in childhood of not talking about problems and trying to avoid anything negative was what she used during most of her marriage. She was married for three years before separating. When I first talked to her, the divorce was pending.

VERONICA

Veronica's parents maintained traditional gender roles complicated by her father's drinking.

My dad, I believe, was an alcoholic. . . . I hated my dad. . . . Everything had to always be his way. If we were watching a TV program, he'd come in and not even act like we were in there. He'd just go and turn what he wanted on. It was like, you know, my mother waited on him hand and foot like I did with my husband. Fixing him dinner, doing this, doing that, so I can see where the similarities are.

He [her husband] acts a lot like my dad. It was just like my dad never played with us, my dad was a very hard worker and he worked real hard so that we could have things, but as far as being there for me, emotionally, my dad was never there. My mom was and I really loved my mom.

In her relationships before she met her husband, Veronica explained,

it just seems the guys that were good for me, I didn't really like. Because I remember dating this pilot who would have given me the shirt off his back. He would have done anything for me. He was so in love with me and I could have cared less. Yet I'm attracted to these people who are outgoing, who are pushy, who feel real confident about themselves. That's a big red flag for me right now.

Of her courtship with her husband, she said,

He is so charming, you wouldn't believe it. So, so charming and I think maybe that's why I was so drawn to him and wanted that relationship because I knew how nice he could be.

During childhood, Veronica learned that everything had to be the man's way; in return, he would provide for physical but not emotional needs. That pattern of relationship was maintained in her marriage. When I met Veronica, she was planning to end her marriage of almost twenty years as soon as her home was sold. In her forties, Veronica is a capable professional who would rather be home with her two children than out supporting them as a single mother.

JEANNIE

There was never quite enough money or attention in Jeannie's family, and what there was went to her brother. During her childhood,

I always remember having very low self-esteem. I always remember being unhappy, but when I look back on it now, those were problems that came from me. I don't really think my parents instilled those in me. Somewhere along the line they had to, but I can't place any one thing on it. I do know that it seemed that whatever my brother did got attention. He was the oldest, he was looked up to.

They would have helped me do anything I wanted, but I never asked because . . . it was always the money. We don't have the money for this, we don't have the money for that. My dad drove a concrete truck and there were a lot of times in the winter when he didn't work. I feel like if I had been pushed harder in school, I would have done better. I wouldn't have just gotten by.

My father was abusive to my mother verbally. They argued in front of us. Sometimes it was just a bickering back and forth. . . . He would drink a lot and come home and abuse her in that way—mostly criticizing, debating issues. . . . He didn't abuse her verbally the way my ex-husband abused me.

Jeannie met her ex-husband right after high school.

When I was a teenager, there was a certain place where everyone met. I met him [her ex-husband] there. Everyone sat in their cars and talked. It was summer, I was seventeen and had just graduated from high school. We were basically the same age. He told me that he would call me.

We dated probably for almost a year. When we were already engaged, I became pregnant and we got married. We lived in his apartment. The abuse started after we were married.

Jeannie is an attractive, bright, expressive person who talks openly about her life and her feelings. A homemaker during the first part of her twenty-year marriage, Jeannie developed a career when she began to realize the marriage might not last and she would have to support herself. Although Jeannie is only slightly overweight, that is the main thing she sees when she looks at herself. Instead of enjoying her charm and vivacity, her husband criticized her about her size constantly. Her weight became his excuse for criticizing and not wanting to be close to her: "If you weren't so fat then I would . . ."

BETTY

Betty is the middle child between two brothers. As a child, she was responsible for helping her parents, each of whom had a serious physical limitation. Betty was sexually abused by a male relative when she was five and by a female relative when she was a preteen.

Betty's first marriage ended in divorce after four years. Betty described her ex-husband as "controlling, he was always putting me down." She said, "I didn't think much of myself. I wasn't going to pick anyone who was going to be healthy for me 'cause I wasn't healthy." She remarried soon after the divorce to a man who "had extramarital relationships all the time, and I still took him back. The final straw was when he kind of backhanded me and broke my nose. When it got to physical abuse, I ended it. I would take emotional, but not physical abuse."

Betty dated her current husband several years before marrying him. In her late forties, Betty has appealing, fresh, natural good looks. She describes herself as being overweight. Before this marriage, Betty did secretarial work in a professional office, but she has two children and has not worked outside of her home during this marriage. Betty is still in her eighteen-year marriage. As a child, her role was caretaker; in her marriage, she maintains this position.

LAURA

As a child, Laura felt close to her mother but knew her unexpressive father loved her. Her mother went to work when Laura was in grade school.

Mom and dad worked different shifts so we were never left with a babysitter. I was always real, real close to my mom and she was close with my brother, too. Dad, you know, I knew he loved us, but he never expressed it verbally, I mean. But, we always took family vacations and extended families were real big. It seemed like every Sunday we were either going to one grandparent's house or the other.

Laura's parents stayed together for the children and divorced after the children were grown-up.

When I got older, I noticed that mom and dad didn't have a real great marriage. . . . My mom waited for a while until I was out of high school and then apparently she had told Dad that if he didn't change his ways, she was going to leave him. It just got to the point where all he wanted to do was to go out into the garage and work. He didn't want to do anything that mom wanted to do like going out for dinner and dancing. You know, I remember one year we went out for their anniversary with Mom and Dad. They didn't do a lot of things, just them alone. It was always friends or family involved.

When I hit my teenage years, I started noticing a lot of arguing and Dad had a short fuse. . . . I didn't understand it at the time, but now, with what I'm going through, he was verbally abusive with mom. You know, he would say real cruel things. Well, maybe not so much they were cruel things, but it was his tone of voice. He was just a moody person. Like when he worked third shift, he was awful. If we woke him up, he would be a real bear.

Laura met her husband several years after high school. After a long distance romance, they got married.

I just thought he was so charming. He wasn't handsome. He was, I don't know, very articulate and looking back, he's an excellent bullshitter. That's what a lot of that was.

In her late thirties, Laura is a professional, "all-American girl" type woman who has one young child. She was married for twelve years before separating.

ANGELA

Angela grew up in a traditional Hispanic family in which the men dominated and the "women can't do anything for themselves, they don't know how to do anything, they need men to survive." Angela's dad is much older than her mother. Angela remembers her parents fighting all the time.

I remember my mom telling me when I was little, I think I'm going to get a divorce, and I'd cry. After time went on, I remember her staying in the marriage and me thinking why is she in it. My dad would come home, he wouldn't talk to her, he'd go straight in his room and wouldn't talk to anybody. He talked to us, but he didn't talk to her. And I thought that was kind of rejecting, rejecting her. I could see that she wasn't happy, I knew that and I remember praying for them to get a divorce because all they did was fight all the time. So I just stayed in my room whenever they were around so that I wouldn't be in the way of their fighting.

Her parents finally got a divorce after Angela was an adult. Angela says of her father, "I think he always did love my mom, but he never did know how to show it. He was not affectionate. My mom was a very affectionate person and my dad was not. My dad was very distant and very uncommunicative with her."

Angela got scholarships so she could go to college. Her mother supported Angela's wish to go to college away from home, but her father did not.

He didn't want me to leave home. He wanted to keep me there, but I got a few scholarships and there was really no way he could say no. He could have, I guess, but anyway, my mom backed me up all the way. Everytime anything happened, he blamed my mom. "See, she's sick and now we can't do anything because we're not there because you let her go out there."

My mom said, "I don't want you to be like me. I can't get out of this marriage because I don't have an education. I don't have a way to support myself. It's not just if you get a divorce; say your husband dies, say he is incapacitated, you need to get out and work. You have to be able to do that."

Angela is a bright, energetic, vivacious, professional woman. She met her husband in college and married him after she graduated: "I wanted to get away from home cause my dad was very strict." She was married for eight years and has one child.

VICKI

Starting in childhood, Vicki was in a caretaker role.

My family was dysfunctional, nonverbal. My mother was a hypochondriac who didn't have much personal strength. She leaned on doctors. I was in a parenting role with my mother, who was in the hospital about once a year. My mother was nasty to me. I have a brother eighteen months older who has not helped with my parents.

Her mother did not think the family could afford to send Vicki to college, so she went to work after high school. When Vicki was a young woman, marriage was the only accepted option for young women, so even though she wanted to be independent, she got married.

I didn't really want to get married. I loved [her ex-husband] and I was indeed glad that I could marry him, but making that commitment was really tough for me to do. I really wanted to go out and get an apartment and, you know, be independent. I really was not prepared to get married. I wasn't ready for that.

You'd never guess that Vicki was in her early sixties. A successful career woman for the last fifteen years, Vicki was once a full-time housewife and mother. Although very unhappy in her marriage, Vicki thought she couldn't make it on her own and believed that she should stay married for the sake of her three children. She was married for more than thirty-five years before deciding to get a divorce.

MARTHA

Growing up in a rural area, Martha had a normal, happy childhood. She characterized her childhood as "super."

I grew up on a farm. I loved everything outdoors. I really never wanted to live anywhere else but there. I had a very happy childhood. Mom was a little domineering, Dad was kind of quiet, but basically their relationship was okay.

I had very, very good grades in high school. I won a scholarship, which my father would not allow me to accept. His idea was women are only meant to go out and get married and have kids, and yet I never held that against my father because that was just the way that he was raised to believe. That many years ago, that was just the accepted norm.

At that time, women married when they were quite young. Martha was first married after high school to a man several years older.

He was an alcoholic, which I didn't realize before I married him. As I've looked back, in a sense there was a little abusiveness there. It was sort of the "I'm the only thing that is important" type of thing and you're just always in the background. But, I guess, I was really too naive to even really notice it. And yet, by that husband, I felt totally loved.

I remember back when we were first married. He thought it was real cute to tie me to the bed while he went off to town with his dad and [a friend]. He just thought it was funny. But I was so young at the time that I never even considered it abusive. It was just like a cruel joke. And there was just a couple of other little things that just recently have I even really thought about.

I can see, if that marriage had lasted longer, it may have gotten into more abusiveness. Just sort of the idea that the man is the only thing that is important and you're just here to cook and go to bed with and sort of that type of thing. That's all that was expected of a woman back that long ago.

Martha's marriage deteriorated as her husband's drinking increased.

I knew I had to go to work, which I did. There was a period of time when he quit drinking and things were great. And then his friend came over with a six-pack of beer and he had a beer and it was just totally downhill from there. I got him to go to one AA meeting and he absolutely refused to go back. And then he would be in and out of jail for drinking or getting in fights while he was drunk. I ended up living with a family. They took care of my daughter while I worked.

Then I was pregnant again so I quit my job, went back to my mom's to have the baby, and in the meantime he was in jail. When I left, I went down and paid his fine before I left town. He called me in the hospital after the second baby was born and that was the last time I ever even talked to him.

For a long time, Martha hoped that she would hear from her husband again, but she never did. During that time, she met her second husband, whom she married soon after getting a divorce. "When we were going together, it was, you know, everything's great. He's kind, considerate, thoughtful. We could talk to midnight every night and it was like we had the same goals and dreams."

Martha is a woman in her early sixties who was married for almost forty years before divorcing. She still feels responsible for her husband and has helped when he has been sick. She describes the marriage as being painful from the beginning. Although Martha stayed home with her children during most of the marriage, she went back to work about fifteen years ago. In her life, Martha moved from a very traditional understanding of women's roles to being an independent career woman.

REBECCA

Rebecca remembers her parents as always critical of her. As a child,

I grew up in a dysfunctional family. I couldn't show my emotions. I couldn't talk about anything or get mad. I was considered the black sheep. I'd do whatever I was told. They said I would listen to anyone and would never use my brain.

During high school, I became really rebellious, drinking and using drugs. The more they talked, the more rebellious I became. I had a dual life. At home I was quiet, submissive, and went to church. When I was away, I was rebellious. I was two people; I didn't know who I was.

My parents never listened to me. When I was [a teenager], I was raped and became pregnant. I had been dating a fellow from my church that my family liked. He had beaten me, but my mother just said, "You must have provoked it." She wouldn't let me go to counseling. They forbid me to talk to anybody about the rape. They decided I should have an abortion.

I tried to commit suicide. I took an overdose of barbiturates.

When her parents found her after the suicide attempt, they woke her up and told her brother to take her to a movie. When I asked Rebecca more about this, she began to cry, disclosing,

I was not supposed to talk about any of my pains so I just shoved everything down. I existed but didn't exist.

I lived at home during college and worked in the health and counseling service. There was one counselor I liked, so I made an appointment with him. I was involved in setting up their peer counseling groups and took a lot of counseling classes. My mother is paranoid about counseling. She said, "I hope nobody sees you go into the counseling center."

Rebecca married shortly after completing college.

That marriage was never any good. I found out on our wedding night that he was gay. When I couldn't take it anymore, I got out.

I had a real hard time dealing with the divorce, and so I wasn't feeling real positive or self-confident then. In some ways I was feeling better 'cause I was away from [her first husband] and that situation and I was in my own apartment for the first time. And that felt really nice to be able to live on my own and do that. But emotionally I was real confused and upset. I was real angry—well, not angry, but I didn't believe in divorce. I had a real struggle with that and the church. So I didn't feel very strong emotionally.

Rebecca met her ex-husband in college. Although he was older than she is, they graduated together. He was married then and had grown children. Rebecca said she knew their marriage would not work out but finally just gave in to the pressure to get married.

I avoided a long time, getting involved with [her ex-husband] 'cause we had been friends a long time and it was just very platonic friends and I knew it wouldn't work out. He always said he wanted to marry me and that was his intent for all the years that I knew him. And I felt very strong that I didn't want to do that.

I remember exactly the day that I just kind of gave up. I don't know how to describe it. It's just like my will to fight left and I was tired of fighting with this guy all the time and kind of resigned myself that that was the best I could do, I guess I didn't deserve any better. . . . I've seen it in my mom, it comes across that you never get what you want and don't expect anything good because you're not going to get it, just kind of settle for whatever you can find 'cause it's the best you'll ever do. I guess that's just what I kind of felt.

Then once I lost the will to fight, it just kind of went from there and we got married. Then I was kind of living in real high denial, you know. Things were wonderful and great and isn't life a bowl of cherries and I'm married. I think that was a lot of it, 'cause I can still remember the feeling. I picture kind of letting my shoulders sloop and just kind of, okay, you win, let's go and get it over with kind of thing.

Then once I did that, it was like these walls I've built. I thought, nobody's going to make this turn out bad. I've got to make this work. Since I had just gotten through a divorce and how traumatic that was for me, it was like I can't go through another one. There's no way. How ungodly that would be to have to go through another divorce. I know with the divorce I lost my hair and was just a real physical mess and I didn't want to go through that again. It was kind of proving to my family that, you know, I am capable of being married and having a good life and that kind of stuff.

I kind of went into it with, well, this is what I'm resigned to so this is what I'll put up with and I'll make the best of it. I'll be happy. . . . It was kind of like, "Well, okay, I'll make myself love you whether I do or not." And I did that really well, or I told myself that I did.

Rebecca has such an open, honest approach to people that she is very easy to like. In her thirties, she is a college graduate and the mother of two young children. In childhood, Rebecca learned to be compliant and submissive, to keep her feelings in, and to settle for whatever was offered to her. These lessons are part of what led her to accept an abusive marriage. She was married almost three years before separating. When I first met with Rebecca, her divorce was pending.

SUMMARY

These women come from widely different backgrounds, ranging from poverty to affluence and from severe abuse to loving families. Twelve of the participants described their fathers as being psychologically abusive to their mothers, but only one of their parents' marriages ended in divorce before the children left home. Fourteen women described their mothers as living in traditional gender positions; one mother's serious level of psychopathology and alcoholism dominated her behavior. Eleven of the participants described their fathers as emotionally unavailable.

Of these eleven, six felt neglected by both parents. Three were physically abused and five sexually abused as children. Alcoholism was a problem in four of the families. As children, six of the women had to take care of their parents. Only three of the participants described childhoods in which their families adequately met their emotional needs. Four of the women were pregnant when they got married.

The diversity in their backgrounds reflects the diversity one might expect in a group of sixteen people. That most of their mothers were in traditional gender roles and most of their fathers emotionally unavailable could be said of any group of women in this age range. The level of psychological abuse in their parents' marriages seems high; but there are no figures to judge this against. Maybe in patriarchal societies psychological abuse is the norm rather than the exception. The levels of alcoholism and physical and sexual abuse are also somewhat higher than is believed to be normal.

All but three of these women described not having a close relationship with either of their parents. They either felt that they had to take care of their parents or that their parents just were not interested, able, or willing to offer them time, attention, or recognition. The pain related to neglect and lack of close emotional connections and support stands out as most closely related to ending up in a psychologically abusive marriage. As children, most of these women often "felt like nobody," like they were "just not there," as described by Karen, the young woman whose poem begins this chapter. As young women, they had little self-confidence and craved loving attention so they were vulnerable to accepting the first love relationship available to them. As you will hear in the following chapters, in spite of their diversity, the stories of their marriage relationships are very similar.

3

CONTROL AND DOMINATION

With him, everything had to be just perfect. It was his way or no way. I had to accept it. I didn't know any other way. (43-year-old hair stylist)

In this chapter, the descriptions of psychological abuse in physically abusive relationships will be compared with descriptions from psychologically abusive relationships, and the similarities between these two types of relationships will be shown. A core theme in both types of relationships is domination and control by the husband. Many studies (e.g., Dobash and Dobash 1979; Jones and Schechter 1992; Ptacek 1988) have shown that domestic violence grows out of male dominance and the need to control. Control and domination are also central qualities in psychologically abusive relationships (Murphy and Casardi 1993) in which the husband holds almost all the power and uses this power to control his wife.

ABUSE OF POWER

Psychological abuse grows out of male sense of entitlement to a position of dominance, control, and power. As Jeannie said, "He saw himself as king and ruler." He dominates all aspects of the relationship including money, sex, social life, and her behavior. Laura summarized this theme with, "He's a control freak."

The wife is expected to be obedient and submissive, conforming to his demands and expectations. Kathy reflected, "Our home was like an extension of the office. I'm the big man at the office, you're the secretary. Here's what I want done."

Walker's (1979) study of physically abusive relationships associates psychological abuse with behavior that is coercive and manipulative, that is designed to promote self needs and neglect the needs of others. All the women pinpointed domination as central in psychological abuse. Martha's story is particularly clear.

Before I went back to work, we only had one car and, of course, it was always his on the weekends to do his hobbies. Our older daughter won a scholarship to the [name of art school]. She went one Saturday. The next week hunting season started. That was the end of her going to school, 'cause he had to go hunting. I tried to talk to him about it.... His answer was, "By God, I'm going to do what I want to do when I want to do it and to hell with anybody else." That was his answer and that's what he's always done.

Domination is maintained in many ways. The most obvious is verbal assaults and denigration. This behavior includes criticizing, belittling, demeaning, deprecating remarks often said in front of other people such as the couple's children. This behavior seems to be a way of punishing her for not living up to his standards and of keeping her in a submissive position. As a sixty-one-year-old woman said, "He could just say the nastiest, nastiest put-down things." Frequently the verbal attacks involved name calling, the most common being to describe her as stupid, crazy, or fat.

PERFECTIONISTIC DEMANDS

Besides the excessive need to control and the abuse of power, descriptions of psychological abuse of children include unrealistic demands as an element of the abuse (Brassard and Gelardo 1987; Hart and Brassard 1987; Nesbit and Karagianis 1987). This pattern is also true in psychological abuse of women. Each woman in the study gave vivid descriptions of unrealistic demands. As Rebecca put it, "If the house wasn't immaculate, he got mad at me." Amy explained that "he got angry if I didn't have the house cleaned and dinner on the table when he got home. He would yell at me if everything wasn't just perfect. The littlest thing upset him."

Such unrealistic demands are at the level of demanding constant perfection. Kreman (1980) identified that physically battered women try very hard to meet the perfectionistic, sometimes contradictory demands of their husbands. This same behavior is typical in psychologically battered women. Here is how two women described their husbands' perfectionistic demands.

If [ex-husband] didn't like what I was wearing, I would change. I wore my hair the way he wanted me to wear it. I kept the house the way he wanted it done. He wanted his shirts hung one-half inch apart in the closet and I made sure I did it. If I didn't, he took them out of the closet, threw them on the floor, and said that they needed to be rewashed and ironed. . . . He would even tell me when I was to go to bed and when I was to get up. (Carol)

His mom told me it was her fault that [ex-husband] was the way he was, 'cause he's the oldest of five and they always expected him to be perfect. Therefore, [ex-husband] makes no mistakes. He is perfect. And she told me that. He has the same fights with his mom as he has with me over being perfect and not doing things right. (Angela)

ECONOMIC DOMINATION

Economic domination is another aspect of psychological abuse in physically abusive relationships (Shepard 1991; Shepard and Pence 1988; Walker 1979). The husbands require unilateral control over the family finances. In this way, the women are kept in the dependent, childlike position of being given an allowance. This economic abuse includes such things as making it difficult for her to get or keep a job, giving her a small, inadequate allowance (which she generally must ask for), taking her money, not including her in financial decisions, and not giving her information about the family's financial situation (Tolman 1992). Whatever money she has is closely monitored by him; frequently, he is critical of her use of her "grocery money." As Amy recalled,

"He controlled the money. He let me manage it for one week and then said that I screwed everything up so 'you aren't allowed to have any money.' He made the decisions about how money should be spent." Laura recounted,

To make a long story short, he told me, "I am the head of the household. I say we are adding on to this room. This is what we're doing. Discussion over." We're talking $20,000, which we didn't borrow. We drained savings to add on and that was his decision. I had nothing to do with it.

Other women reported similar experiences.

So he was determining what I needed and what I didn't need all the time, from the beginning. I never had a car. (Dorothy)

He had control of money. He would give me money and take money back from me. (Tamika)

I can remember one time I went to a jewelry party and bought a necklace. I thought he was going to have a fit. I never spent money on myself. (Jeannie)

Sometimes it seemed like the women had some control over the money because he would put her in charge for a short time. Carol's story is typical.

There would be such fights over money, arguments constantly over money. I got sick and tired of it. He wanted me to be in control of the checkbook. He gave the checkbook to me. He wanted me to be in charge of it, but when there would be arguments about it I'd say, "Here, you take it if I can't handle it." He refused to take it. He wanted me to keep it. He wanted me to do it, but [ex-husband] was a spender. A lot of times [ex-husband] would write a check or go to the bank machine and not write it down. Things just got to be such a mess. It didn't matter what mistake was made in the checkbook, in the house, with the kids, whatever the mistake was, it was my fault and I was supposed to straighten it out. On numerous occasions I would cry that I don't want to take care of this checkbook anymore. "You take care of it and then you can handle it the way you want." He refused to take it back. I think it was a controlling thing. It was something he could yell at me about.

SEXUAL DOMINATION

Control of a couple's sexual relationship has also been discussed as a psychologically abusive element in physically abusive relationships (Tolman 1992). This is also true in psychologically abusive relationships. His needs are all important and her needs and feelings are ignored; she is expected to be subservient, to have sex whenever and however he wants it. Carol said, "I would just cry the whole time. I think he enjoyed the crying." Listen to how other women described their sexual relationships.

He was sexually dominating. That was one of the top two reasons that I left him. He was raping me. It all started in [the year before they separated]. We hadn't had sex for a long time. I hated him. I didn't want to be near him. He just started forcing me whenever he wanted sex. I tried to stop him, but he held me down. He wasn't that big, but he was strong. I cried and he just said that everything would be okay. I stayed for another year after that started. (Amy)

He wanted to go to bed at 8:00 on Saturday night. He'd get mad if I didn't just want to go jump in bed with him and here's a little child running around us. I'd say, "Well, you know, I have to put her to bed." He didn't even want to wait to have sex until I could get her in bed. No, if I couldn't do it right now, when he wants it, then to hell with me. (Becky)

Sometimes I felt like he raped me. Sometimes when I said, "Well, I just don't like it," he would say, "Well, you just have to meet my needs." And I just said, "Okay, just do whatever you want" and I'd just lay there like a limp rag. (Veronica)

He was always pushing for sex. I used to hide from him. He said, "You have to do this for me" and would become mean and angry. (Betty)

He often wanted anal sex, but I couldn't stand it. He also had lots of toys. Sometimes I'd end up crying, but he usually pushed me ahead anyway. Then he would say, "I'll never do it again," but he would. He couldn't live without it for one day. I learned to dread and hate for the night to come. (Rebecca)

SOCIAL ISOLATION AND HUMILIATION

Another area of control relates to the couple's activities with others. Social isolation gradually develops as a result of the husband's extreme possessiveness. Dobash and Dobash (1979), Ferraro (1988), Martin (1976); Pagelow (1981), Tolman (1989), and Walker (1979, 1984) identify this behavior as central in physically abusive relationships. The husband tries to control when she goes out, who she sees, who she talks to, what she does, and where she goes. All her outside contacts are limited. The husband experiences time spent with others, even family members, as an indication that she prefers them over him and responds with sullenness, irritability, criticism, and verbal attacks (Ferraro 1988).

This pattern of controlling social contacts and criticizing her friends and family is evident also in psychologically abusive relationships. Tammi disclosed, "I had cut off all contact with anybody 'cause he got mad. He'd yell, 'Who in the fuck are you talking to now?' " Dorothy's story is similar. "I became isolated from my family. . . . He would say, 'Those people are so screwed up.' " Debbi divulged, "He didn't like any of my friends. Something was wrong with every one of them. He would take it as a real personal offense if I chose to do anything with any of them."

The need to isolate the woman from her friends and family often led to moving to another part of the country.

We moved away to get away from our families. He said they were evil, that they don't love us. At one point I believed him because he had so many good reasons. Every time they would come over he would be nice but then be critical as soon as they left. He was mean and rude to his own family. (Amy)

After we got married, he immediately took me far away from my family and friends. He decided who I could be friends with. (Laura)

Often jealousy is involved. In physically abusive relationships, "fear of a wife's promiscuity may be so strong that husbands fantasize lovers and develop paranoid perceptions of their wives' intentions. This leads to excessively controlling behavior" (Ferraro 1988, 133). The same behavior is true in psychologically abusive relationships. The women reported that if they went out with women friends or talked to neighbors, their husbands accused them of looking for another man. This possessiveness and jealousy led to behavior such as his monitoring and tracking all her social contacts.

He never wanted to go out with me to do things with friends. He was always too tired. He'd say, "All you want to do is find another guy." He is still accusing me of running around and I never did. (Amy)

And he was just real jealous, you know. . . . The neighbor next door, I couldn't even talk. . . . Every time I saw him or he came over for some reason, I was flirting. (Rebecca)

Acting in humiliating ways in social situations is another way of controlling (Walker 1979). The women in this study reported that the rare occasions when their husbands agreed to go to social events were usually painful because their husbands either acted in embarrassing ways, such as getting drunk, or neglected or denigrated them; Debbi and Vicki both felt embarrassed when their husbands became drunk at social events. The husbands' negative behavior, however, was often not related to drinking; the men generally were pleasant to other people but were often critical of and belligerent to their wives, even in public.

I recall one time when we were playing a card game with my family. It was Hearts. He was collecting all the hearts and I stopped him. I didn't do it intentionally. I had the card to do it. I thought he was going to kill me. I thought he was just going to kill me. He was so mad, I mean I was almost in tears. He embarrassed me so much because he kept saying, "That was just luck, there was no skill to that. You knew I was trying to get all of them." I've never played the game since. (Jeannie)

"CHARMING BUT PHONY"

Although the husbands might humiliate their wives in public or social situations, these men were also able to act in appealing and likable ways to others. The women described them as "charming but phony." This engaging behavior was used to get recognition or support for his view of himself.

He needs somebody, he has to tell them how great he is. You know, I'm involved in the Chamber, and I'm involved in this, and I'm, and I'm, and I'm. He tries to impress people. . . . He was never satisfied no matter how good people told him he was. He was just never satisfied. (Veronica)

The relationships he has with people, like his brother, he really doesn't have that many friends, close friends. It's always when he needs something that he goes to these people and gets it and then that's it. . . . He'll never have any kind of caring relationship with them. It's whenever he needs something, then he searches out for somebody. (Debbi)

The women described their husbands as egocentric, charming but phony, self-centered, and fake. The image is of a narcissist, a person who requires excessive attention and admiration, who feels entitled to special treatment, who exploits others to indulge self, who lacks empathy, and who disregards the rights and needs of others. "Narcissism inevitably includes a desire to encompass everything, the me and the not-me, the desired object and the eschewed object" (Bernstein and Freedman 1993, 4). This need to encompass, control, dominate is central for these men.

He's just basically a selfish person—an "I, me, and I'm first" type. He thinks he's smarter than everybody else. He's smart, but he's not smarter than everybody else, and not in all the ways of life. He ridicules people. I think that's why he doesn't have a whole lot of friends. He's better than everybody and why be bothered with them. (Kathy)

I don't really think he's capable of a loving, open relationship. He's very narcissistic. You know, his mother is real narcissistic. She's like a little girl who is demanding attention and she's cute, in her own way, but after a while it gets real irritating. I see him as kind of that way and it's—all of his aches and pains and body things that are going on—it's for attention. (Betty)

He thinks he is entitled to be taken care of, to be the ruler, to criticize anyone who does not please him. As one woman said,

"His world revolves around his wants and needs, and mine are never going to be met." There is little understanding or support for the wife and almost constant attempts to control and dominate her.

Psychological abuse invites increasing dependency and fear while reducing self-esteem (Murphy and Casardi 1993). Psychologically abusive relationships are characterized by high negative or abusive behavior and low positive or kind behavior. The polarities of domination and submission and aggression and passivity pervade all aspects of the relationship. One partner keeps the other partner subordinate using negative reinforcement, verbal attacks, and withdrawal of attention. In chapter 4, I will show how these polarities are built into our patriarchal society.

4

BECAUSE WE ARE WOMEN

It was always, "Oh, you're a girl, you can't do that. You can't play sports. You have to cook and clean and do laundry." When it comes to doing all this other stuff, you know, you're not capable of doing that. And so I think a lot of that came from my mom, 99 percent of it came from her, that you have to have a man. (32-year-old secretary)

I waited on him [her husband] hand and foot, I know I did. I know I waited on him a lot and in the beginning I think he was fairly independent because his mom had died early and all that. I don't know why, probably because of the way my mother was. You know, my mom waited on my dad hand and foot. (44-year-old nurse)

Looking at psychological abuse through the lenses of feminist theory and critical theory, it can be explained as an exaggeration of patriarchy's usual positioning of men as dominant and women as submissive and subservient. Feminist critical analysis has exposed the connections between violence, authoritarianism, masculinity, and patriarchy, a social system of male power and dominance (Hartmann 1976: Yllö 1993). Patriarchal societies have socially constructed gender hierarchies that ensure unjust power relationships and male oppression of women (Yllö 1993). This "institutionalized system of male domination and privilege is the mechanism that ensures women's subordination" (Bricker-

Jenkins and Hooyman 1989, 9) and creates the conditions necessary for abuse. An understanding of patriarchy and an analysis of gender helps explain why women accept psychological abuse.

A basic premise of patriarchal law, religion, philosophy, and morality is that men are superior to women and therefore have the responsibility and the right to control the public sphere of business and government and the private realm of the family (Coltheart 1986). In patriarchal societies, power is experienced as a finite commodity that controls the distribution of rights, resources, and opportunities (Van Den Bergh and Cooper 1986) and is used to repress women (White and Epston 1990) and other minorities. Patriarchy is both a structure in which men have more power and privileges and an ideology that legitimizes this structure. In patriarchal societies, women are expected to be obedient to men in exchange for protection and security (Ferraro 1988). The control and domination that characterize psychologically abusive relationships can be seen as an extension of the gender duality that characterizes patriarchy.

GENDER AND MALE DOMINANCE

Gender relations establish two types of persons, men and women, each gender with different traits and capacities. Although sexual characteristics and attributes are continuous, not dichotomous (Money 1973), individuals are divided into males or females and then taught from birth how to live out that assigned category (Kaschak 1992). Sex is a biological category and gender is a socially constructed category, involving the assignment of certain tasks and descriptive adjectives to each gender (Butler 1990; Norman 1980). Since biological sex is easily confused with socially prescribed gender roles, gendered behavior is assumed to be unavoidable and natural (Goodrich et al. 1988); however, each society develops unique concepts of what are essential characteristics of each gender (Goffman 1977). These characteristics inevitably involve repression of similarities and accentuation of differences between the genders (Flax 1990b), with masculine and feminine being defined in opposition, against each other (Flax 1990a).

Gender is not an interior state of being; it is a performance, a way of acting and doing (Butler 1990; Minnich 1990), involving learned behavior, feeling, thinking patterns. In patriarchies, gender places men in the dominant position and women in the subordinate, precluding the possibility of equality and reciprocity between the sexes and narrowing the range of possible behaviors for both sexes (Goodrich et al. 1988). As deBeauvoir (1961) stated, "one is not born a woman, but rather becomes one" (301). "Gender determines women's oppression more significantly than does biology. Whatever might be her position in the world and whatever her individual accomplishments, a woman is appraised first as a woman, and only afterward for her position or accomplishments" (Young 1990b, 75).

The study of gender relations and gender differentiation includes all aspects of women's experiences: their subjectivities, their situations, and their domination (Flax 1990a). Gender identity governs much of human life, requiring certain behaviors and forbidding others. Gender systems include: (1) two dichotomous exclusionary categories that exaggerate differences and suppress similarities, (2) a division of labor based on gender differentiation, and (3) social regulation of sexuality that supports heterosexual pairs (Mitchell 1966; Norman 1980; Rubin 1975; Thorne 1982). Gender concepts, relations, and systems differentiate men from women, establish that they will desire the other, and give men "powers over women that women do not have over ourselves or men" (Minnich 1990, 143). Gender identifies a woman's appropriate personality, behavior, and emotions as the opposite or mirror image of a man's, determines a woman's place in the world, and pervades every aspect of her functioning (Bernstein and Freedman 1993). Kaschak (1992) identifies that "every aspect of experience, from our first moments, is gendered" (5–6).

Even the word "woman" has been a relational sign, as in the sentence "I now pronounce you man and wife," which was common in wedding ceremonies. The woman is identified as wife, not a person but a dependent. "She is defined and differentiated with reference to man and not he with reference to her; she is the incidental, the inessential as opposed to the essential. He is the Subject, he is the Absolute—she is the Other" (deBeauvoir 1961, xvi).

In all societies, the duality of Self and Other is established. The group identified as Subject or Self describes and distinguishes the Other in reference to itself. In patriarchal societies, woman is situated as other, as less than or inadequate, as observed object, constantly being watched and watching herself, trying to hide her inadequacy and powerlessness (Gardiner 1985). Starting from this basic position, women have little option other than to accept as reality negative evaluations from men, who inevitably are seen as the authority (Gallop 1985). Even those who fight against these evaluations may at the same time accept them as part of their way of observing self.

As the dominant structural force in this country, capitalist patriarchy plays an important part in the creation of self. In patriarchal societies, dominance and control are central aspects of the masculine sense of self and are considered inappropriate and unfeminine for women (Ferraro 1988). An analysis of gender polarity shows that gender underlies dualisms such as autonomy and dependency, dominant and submissive, strong and weak (Benjamin 1988; Goodrich et al. 1988).

When I brought up the topic of men's and women's roles in our society in the final group meeting with the women, many of them had a clear understanding of the role of patriarchy and gender in their personal relationships. Tamika's dissection of women's role in giving men power is particularly striking.

There is a belief system that says that the male is supposed to be the authority figure. There was a part of me that worked at making him the authority even though intuitively I knew that he was not the authority. It was like a constant progression of giving up power to make him, to elevate him, to make him this real figurehead. That it is right for him to have the power.

A lot of that goes on in the African American community even today. If you listen to African American women or the nationalist type of Afrocentric woman, you hear that we have to work to make the black man the male. We have to give him the power. We have to elevate him.

I don't think that's so different than that unconscious belief system that is interwoven in the patriarchal system. I think that's the belief that's interwoven in that system, and somehow we come into it and believe that it exists. We constantly affirm it in ourselves and we affirm it in our male children. We constantly want that to be our reality until one day we wake up and say, "God, I'm not listening to what's really coming from me," 'cause a part of me is saying, "No, that's not real." I think that's where the insanity comes from. It's like this inner conflict—this inner conflict constantly going on in a war against myself. I'm trying to make this a reality and once I stop making that a reality, I found out that I can be my own woman.

Tammi was also very insightful about society's role in the domination of women.

To me, it goes back to the way society has got it structured. The society is structured, and always has been, by white males. That is the way it is and I believe that's the way it's going to stay at least until I die. They rule and control everything. This is a political type of thing, but I believe it. And I also believe that we've been brainwashed. I think women and society and men also are just brainwashed.

The society makes it that way. It's okay what he does. It's always been that way from the beginning of time when the caveman was pulling us around by our hair, you know. He's the boss.

I think the reason they get away with it is because they're men. Men get away with a lot of things in society because it's okay for them to be that way, to do that, to talk down to women, to be one step up, to be over women, to dominate.

These women understood that the domination and control which are central in psychological abuse are a pervasive part of our society. In capitalist patriarchal societies, all women experience some type of disadvantage, mistreatment, fear of attack, or lack of power. The difference between the women in this study and other women is the degree or extent of abuse experienced.

GENDER SOCIALIZATION

Feminine or masculine identity and gender relations are learned by the way one is treated by parents, grandparents, siblings, teachers, and so on (Money and Erhardt 1972; Tavris 1992). As gender is learned, this oppressive system is internalized so that by the time women marry, they are generally self-demanding and self-critical; without realizing it, they have learned to participate in their own oppression. Although the experience of gender relations varies by culture, race, and class and changes over time (Flax 1990a), in patriarchies gender always establishes women as object, as opposite from men and subjugated by men. Gender socialization was an important factor in how the women in this study constructed their identities and positions in relation to men.

My dad was the breadwinner. He was the authoritarian figure. My mother, yes, she was supposed to keep the kids. I mean do what the kids needed to do and make dinner. (Dorothy)

Mom played very ignorant, that she can't do anything at all unless Daddy was around or a man to do it. Women just weren't capable of changing a light bulb or cleaning this or doing that. She just played the real helpless victim all the time. (Rebecca)

I went from my parents' house to his house and I was just used to cleaning up everything. You know, if there are dishes, you go do the dishes. It was just natural. That's what my mother had taught me to do, so that's what I did. (Becky)

The construction of any totality requires the suppression of differences. All related qualities are included in the construction, and all other qualities are part of the opposite pole (Young 1990b). Those qualities not identified with man become the constructed woman. Using this phallocentric logic, relational difference becomes binary opposition, with the elements of the polarity organized in a rigid hierarchy. In a phallocentric society, language and ideology create masculine as strong, rational, and powerful, and feminine as other, weak, emotional, irrational, and powerless, in need of protection and shelter. Men are accorded the more aggressive and expansive qualities and women the more confining and vulnerable ones (Kaschak 1992). Women are located and identified in a position of vulnerability to abuse, and men are located in a position to be able to be abusive.

In traditional patriarchal families, young women learn strict directives that require them to be flexible, obedient, and pleasing. Girls are expected to be good and to be controlled (Brown and Gilligan 1992), believing they cannot control the circumstances of their lives (Walker 1979). They learn that their worth depends on their beauty and appeal to men and not on what they achieve and how effectively and creatively they manage their lives. Becoming a feminine-gendered person has meant limiting oneself to a dependent, passive, and/or childlike position (Bernstein 1993).

Women have been discouraged from being aggressive or independent except in the service of others such as their children. Their ideal was the all-giving, idealized mother known only to infants (Bernstein 1993). Traditional husbands support this unrealistic image of what their wives should be and do. Here are two women's comments about being treated like a child.

The pattern was that if I was good by his standards then he would give me something, usually something material, but sometimes some of his time. I had to earn time, a relationship with him, based on meeting his standards.

A year ago he had asked me what I wanted. I said I would like us to take a trip. We had the trip all planned, but then, at the last minute, he said he wouldn't take me because he thought we weren't getting along. (Debbi)

When he wanted to get his point across, he would get right up in my face with his finger and shake it in my face. I look back and remember how I hated that. He made me feel like a child when he did that. And I've seen him do that with my kids, too. I can still see that finger shaking. (Carol)

QUALITY OF FEMININITY

Research has shown that high acceptance of femininity is associated with low self-esteem, high anxiety, and low social acceptance (Norman 1980). "Contemporary research on sex roles has found that attributes labeled as feminine are demeaned by men and women and hence are less socially desirable to both sexes" (Wetzel 1981, 11). In a classic study, Broverman, Broverman, and Clarkson (1970) found that a group of psychologists identified traits such as objective, logical, independent, active, decisive, adventurous, self-confident, direct, worldly, and ambitious with healthy adult males. Traits such as emotional, subjective, home oriented, sensitive to others' feelings, intuitive, submissive, gentle, and expressive were associated with healthy adult females. Unfortunately for women, the traits of a healthy male were seen as identical with the traits of a healthy adult. Historically women have had to choose between being healthy adults and being feminine adults. Sadly, many of those who chose health were labeled unfeminine and deviant even by mental health professionals (Norman 1980).

When asked to describe themselves during the time they were in abusive relationships, the women choose words traditionally identified as feminine. The positive words they used included nurturing, tolerant, adapted, patient, caring, giving, accepting, loyal, kind, trusting, loving, forgiving, hard working, naive, trusting, obedient, peacekeeper, unselfish, reliable, hopeful, faithful, responsible, friendly, diligent, thoughtful, trustworthy, and faithful; it sounds like something I was taught in Girl Scouts. Think about the words that are not used, like: successful, powerful, competent, effective, intelligent, sexy, fun loving, happy, playful. The negative words they used also fit the traditional stereotype: passive, vulnerable, revengeful, manipulative, hopeless, lost, lonely, hurt, confused, sad, anxious, fearful, worthless, used, abused, neglected, insecure, downcast, martyr, defensive, ill, cynical, depressed, sarcastic, resentful, self-destructive, isolated, weak, unstable. None chose words associated with any of the traits identified as describing healthy adult males. While in psychologically abusive relationships, these women agreed that qualities such as objective, logical, independent, active, decisive, adventurous, self-confident, direct, worldly, and ambitious are reserved for men.

TAKING CARE OF OTHERS

Women are taught that it is selfish to think of their needs and wants; their self-esteem is based on self-sacrifice (Kaschak 1992). Within the family, women are encouraged "to seek satisfaction in constantly deferring to men and to men's definition of what they should be" (Weedon 1987, 40). Part of women's role is physically and emotionally to care for their husbands. This caring "involves stepping out of one's own personal frame of reference into the other's" (Nodding 1984, 24).

Becoming engrossed in their husbands, women often give up their own interests and own sense of reality, of what is important, and assimilate the world according to the men (Bartky 1990; Nodding 1984). Some participants gave up their careers in order to take care of their husbands. Others continued their careers and took care of their children and husbands. Jeannie described this pattern: "I could work as long as I could still take care of everything at home and the kids. What it really boiled down to was as long as he wasn't inconvenienced, I could work."

The participants saw it as their responsibility to take care of him, giving up their own interests to put him first.

As the children became of school age, I became very involved on church and school committees. I was very careful about not letting it affect [ex-husband's] life in any way. I would get up extra early and clean the house and make sure everything was in order. I felt I was a good leader, organizer, and a good Christian example of a wife. [Her ex-husband] never encouraged these things, but if they began to interfere in any way, he would be critical. Anything that he criticized or complained about, in the least little way, I quickly dropped out of. If [her ex-husband] didn't think it was okay, then I avoided it like the plague.

He wanted me to be here [at home]. I went on the Women's Retreat two years in a row. I was so depressed both times that I went on it. I came back and got so much hell for it that I refused to go anymore. I would make excuses for not going because I didn't want to tell them that [her ex-husband] didn't like it. . . . It was easier not to go than to have to deal with him when I did go, so I stopped going. (Carol)

I'm the kind of person that I care more for others. I care for myself a lot, but I'm a very caring person. I'm the kind of person that my dream is to go to like Ethiopia and help the children out, help the people out there. That's the kind of person I am. I'm a very giving person to other people, and he knows that. . . . He uses his pain to get you to take care of him. (Amy)

Receiving the care and attention of women is seen as an entitlement by men, but they often fail at being attentive to women. Psychologically abusive relationships are one-sided. She understands, she works to improve the relationship, she is giving. This imbalance confirms to both of them her inferior position in the hierarchy of gender (Bartky 1990).

It didn't matter what I wanted, it didn't matter. After my daughter was born, I was very, very sick with the flu and he wanted to go snowmobiling. He got mad and cussed me out and took off on his snowmobile anyway and left me there with a baby. (Becky)

I wasn't getting any positive reinforcement at home. I couldn't do anything right whether it was in bed or cooking. You know, I never got any kind word. I never got any kind words. All the things that I've done, and all the community service I've done, all the awards I got, you know, I got statues and certificates. I didn't ever get one that's really good according to [her ex-husband]. (Dorothy)

As long as I did not disagree with him, it was fine. If I had any problems or if I was upset about anything, he had something that was always worse than mine. (Jeannie)

I always referred to him as a guest in my home. He lived there, but we never did anything as a family. So when he left, it really wasn't devastating, it wasn't lonely. I was lonely when he was there. I think that is the worst kind of loneliness is to have someone who is physically there, but he's not there. (Debbi)

GENDER ROLES AND IDEOLOGIES

Gender roles identify types of work each gender performs. The following three beliefs undergird patriarchal gender roles in the United States: (1) women need men, (2) women are responsible for problems in relationships, (3) men have the right to control women (Goodrich et al. 1988). So female roles are generally passive, requiring subjugating one's own needs to the needs of another (Norman 1980). Traditionally, the main work of women has related to assisting, serving, pleasing, and caring for others. In women, self-denial and self-effacement are valued qualities.

Today there are three main types of gender ideologies: traditional, a "cookies and milk mom"; egalitarian, a "career woman"; and transitional, "super mom," a woman who tries to do it all. Each of these gender roles includes a gendered ego-ideal, conscious and unconscious behavior rules, emotional practices (which feelings to express and which to suppress), and guidelines about balance of power and division of labor (Hochschild 1990). Women in psychologically abusive relationships generally begin marriage in the "cookies and milk mom" role, trying to keep her husband and children happy. As the marriage progresses, the women sometimes move to the "super mom" role, still trying to keep husband and children happy and also develop a career.

In relation to gender roles and ideologies, psychological abuse follows the patterns established in physical abuse, i.e., it is more common in families in which men and women follow traditional gender ideology and in families in which husband and wife disagree about which gender ideology to follow (Bepko 1989; Coleman and Straus 1986). Studies of battered women indicate that a major reason for violence is that the woman failed to live up to his expectations of a good wife (Dobash and Dobash 1979) and that violence is more prevalent in husband-dominant couples (Yllö 1984) and in traditional patriarchal men (Smith 1990; Telch and Lindquist 1984; Walker 1979).

All the participants in this study described traditional gender roles. She took care of the children and the family and he was the principal breadwinner. She had the family responsibility and he had the power.

The thing was, he didn't do anything for the kids. I took care of them. (Carol)

All roles for women have been very limiting. You take care of the males. The women did all the care-taking. It was always there what our roles were. As women, you were supposed to do. (Tamika)

He never helped with [their sons]. He never did any kind of household thing because that was women's work. [Her ex-husband] was a guest, absolutely a guest. (Dorothy)

I was sick, real sick for a couple of years. He'd come home from the golf course and I'd say, "Would you take the kids to the pool? They've been chomping at the bit to go to the pool." But he never would take them. He just couldn't. He's not patient with children. (Kathy)

When I was pregnant with the twins, [ex-husband] told me that he just couldn't help me. He had a variety of excuses for not being able to help. He was busy with his job, he was opening a new real estate office. During my pregnancy he was gone a lot and drinking a lot.

I wanted to do things as a family, but he didn't. He didn't do anything he didn't want to do. He has gone to very few of the children's sports or school events. I had absolute, total, complete responsibility for the children. (Debbi)

I never knew when he was coming home. It wasn't any of my goddamn business. "You've got food to eat and a roof over your head, what else do you want?" That was his attitude.

When the kids were involved in something in school, it was usually I who always went. If he went, he would make sure he would get home just in the nick of time to go. (Jeannie)

[Ex-husband] never wanted to do anything with [their son] even like go to the zoo or go for a walk. He would never do that. So I always felt like the family was just [my son] and me. (Angela)

[Ex-husband] never cooked, never changed diapers. He did do some things to help around the house, those things that he particularly wanted to do. Things were categorized as either women's work or men's work. He did go to [their son's] games, but he never went to any of the girls' school events. . . . He was a nonparticipant in the family. (Vicky)

Basically I went to the grocery store by myself one night during the week. I can't say he would watch them. He would be in the house with them, but he never knew what they were doing 'cause his nose was always in the television set. So I can't say he watched them. And as I say, to go to the grocery store and that was it.

That's just the woman's role, you know. That you're just the mother and a wife, you're not a person. I think that's generally how things have been accepted for years.

It's like his family was supposed to think he was great no matter what he did to them. You're just supposed to take it and forget it, you know. (Martha)

The only time their husbands seemed to be involved with the family was when something one of them accomplished could be used as a positive reflection on him.

The way I see it is we were like the hood ornaments. "Here's my wonderful family. Yes, I'll let my wife be successful and do certain things just to mirror how wonderful I am, but I'm not going to tell her I think she's wonderful." [Their son] was a good athlete. He was captain of the basketball team in high school and all that, but even [their son] was there to make [ex-husband] look good. (Dorothy)

He was participatory, but it was participatory when it suited him. He would always go to Father's Day at school. That's where you're seen; therefore people know that you're a good father. (Kathy)

It's like the only time the kids were there was if they did something in school to brag about or something like that. (Martha)

Studies of men who use violence in relationships show that they generally have traditional ideas about male and female roles, seeing men as dominant, strong, and controlling. The same traditional roles exist in psychologically abusive relationships. Their wives should be submissive and take all the traditional household responsibilities as well as accept the husband's definition of the relationship and preferences with regard to child discipline, sexual activity, and financial management. These men are unreflective about their own needs and feelings. They have particular difficulty with feelings that are not considered masculine, such as tenderness, joy, silliness, dependency, affection, fear, loneliness, and sadness. Many needs are also unacceptable, including dependency, affection, nonsexual touch, support, and assistance. Even stress and anger is not recognized until it has built up (Ferraro 1988). Generally, these men range from adequate to good providers of material things, but they are unable or unwilling to be emotionally giving. Debbi painted a wonderful portrait of this system.

So much that I wanted he was unable to give me, a family and a relationship. I really wanted that. His feeling about what he needed to do in a marriage was to support the family. That was uppermost and that would be monetarily. We were kind of like things that he would buy. He would have a fancy car, he would have children, and he would have a wife and she would wear nice clothes and have nice jewelry and she would, you know, be able to go nice places and make him feel good to do that. To be able to say, "Yeah, my wife can go have lunch and go with her friends and my kids are in swimming and my kids do this and my kids do that." But he was never involved in that. It was like he was managing a company and this is what you do and I'll just sit back and see it all work together. That's how he felt.

Gender is a powerful, socially constructed, all-inclusive reality that is indoctrinated into women and men from birth until death. As women learn to be feminine, they learn to be self-denying and submissive, to serve and care for others. They are rewarded and praised for this behavior, which later makes them vulnerable to mistreatment and psychological abuse (Forward 1986). When you consider how deeply engrained these one-down, submissive positions are, it is amazing that women are ever able to break the model and create another way of living. In fact, "to expect an individual woman on her own to change her part significantly is to ignore the power of socially constructed and socially legitimated reality" (Goodrich et al. 1988, 170).

5

PATTERNS OF ABUSE

I would just try to do better. I never would argue with him.
I would always retreat in tears. . . . I could never win with
him. He complained I never communicated with him, but
whenever I tried to communicate with him, he would always tell me why I was wrong to think that way. And so
it finally reached a point of why bother. You know, I got
tired of listening to him criticize me. (37-year-old nurse)

As explored in the previous chapter, the basic pattern of domi-
nation/submission is a central tenet of our patriarchal society.
This chapter will discuss the five specific interaction patterns that
characterize psychologically abusive relationships. Three or more
of these patterns existed in each of these psychologically abusive
relationships. In each pattern, the abuser interacts at or against
(instead of with) his partner, transforming her into an object toward which he can inflict his emotions. She adapts to him. A
relationship can be defined as psychologically abusive if at least
three of these patterns are constantly present.

PATTERN ONE: "ADJUST YOURSELF"

A committed couple relationship is a complementary and cir-
cular system in which there is continuing mutual influence and
predictable response patterns. Perception of experience is influ-

enced by interpretations of "present and anticipated responses to the current situation, by the relationship they have experienced together historically, and by the ways they have learned and decided to handle such situations in their families of origin" (Massey 1989, 130). In psychologically abusive relationships, his present and anticipated dominant attitude and criticism and her learned patterns of submission, adaptation, and caretaking combine to create the first pattern. Here is how Dorothy explains this pattern.

Well, I didn't verbally question or fight back verbally because he didn't like that and that didn't seem to work. I think that the pattern that was established early and continued on was, "Okay, figure out what's going on here and adjust to it. Adjust yourself, adjust what you're doing, and then things might quiet down."

This interaction pattern, identified by Bateson (1972) as complementary schismogenesis, involves constant adjustment by one partner in response to the other. Schismogenesis is a pattern in which there is progressive differentiation, that is, the distinctions between the two people continually become greater. Complementary differentiation involves contrasting behaviors that evoke each other, such as aggression and submission. In complementary schismogenesis, complementary behaviors promote further differentiation. For example, the more aggressive and dominant he is, the more passive and submissive she becomes. As the pattern continues, smaller and smaller shifts or behavior changes in one partner evoke complementary responses from the other partner. Knowing how verbally attacking he can become, she now does what she thinks he wants even before he glances at her angrily. "This schismogenesis, unless restrained, leads to a progressive unilateral distortion of the personalities, . . . which results in mutual hostility between them and must end in the breakdown of the system" (Bateson 1992, 68). Amy related her experience with this interaction pattern.

He would look at you like that. I just had that feeling and I didn't want to start it. I didn't want to start any problems. It was much easier with him to just go along with what he has to say, because if you don't, you're going to hear about it. Whether he verbally abuses you or he doesn't talk to you for days. He'll just ignore you for days.

PATTERN TWO: DOUBLE BIND

In the second pattern, paradox and contradiction are used to create instability and confusion. The wife learns that she is in a double bind, a situation in which no matter what she does, she cannot win or do it right (Bateson 1972). Since there are two conflicting messages or injunctions, following or believing the primary injunction means not following or believing the second injunction, because the second injunction is the paradoxical opposite of the first injunction. Whether she follows the primary verbal directive or the secondary implied directive, she can be attacked. A double-bind interaction pattern exists when one person is in control and the other person is blocked from clarifying or commenting on the conflicting messages and prohibited from leaving the relationship (Basic 1992).

There are four characteristics of double-bind relationships. First, the relationship is intense rather than casual. Second, there are conflicting messages (Bateson 1972). In psychologically abusive relationships, there are two sets of conflicting messages.

One set of conflicting messages is "I want to be close to you," but "I can't be close to you because there is something wrong with you." Just when she gets one thing right, just the way he wants it, he identifies something else that is wrong with her or with the way she does something. This new flaw is used to prevent closeness between them. All the participants talked about their husbands identifying that the lack of closeness was because of some flaw in the woman.

I got so sick and tired of trying and getting rejected. You begin to think there's so much stuff wrong with you. And I did. I thought there was something wrong with me that he didn't want to be a part of my life. Maybe if I went to school, maybe if I lost weight, maybe if I got a job and paid off all his debts. (Carol)

The last time I lost all the weight, I lost sixty-five pounds. I went on one of those fasting diets. He didn't think I could do it. . . . He confessed that he had been fooling around for five years. Not with the same person, just basic fooling around, and that I had finally done something that he had always wanted and now he wanted to try to make it work. So it's like I'm finally good enough. . . . But then there wasn't any money because I had spent it all. Everything I did that I would try to change, he'd just find something else. There was always something wrong with me. (Jeannie)

The second set of messages is "If you withdraw from me in any way, I will punish you," but "If you reach out to me in any way, I will reject you." Here is how two women were punished if they withdrew.

So I started losing myself. I didn't have much contact with my friends, 'cause I noticed if I talked to them on the phone, he would withdraw affection and attention, wouldn't talk to me, no conversation, no communication. That was my punishment for talking to someone else on the phone. And if I saw my daughter, the same thing, or my grandkids. He'd say, "Oh, you'd rather be with them." And I thought, well, okay [I'll do it your way]. My communication with them [her daughter and grandchildren] was cut off to almost nothing. (Tammi)

He made it so I really didn't want to go, because I didn't want to listen to all the hassles. He was very jealous, so if I went anywhere, I was leaving him behind. He made it so that I just lost contact with most of my friends that I did anything with. (Rebecca)

The punishment for initiating any type of closeness was equally severe.

You never initiated it with [ex-husband]. It had to be initiated by him . . . .Once my friend and I went out and bought a new negligee. It was red. I worked it out so that she [her friend] could take care of the kids and make sure they got to where they needed to go. We had the night to ourselves. I put on the negligee and he got angry. He was so angry. He yelled at me and said, "Nobody will tell me when I'm going to have sex. I will have it when and how and where I want it." It just crushed me, absolutely crushed me. (Carol)

I always had hope. . . . I didn't really want to change him. I just wanted him to participate and to be more loving towards me. That would have made a big difference. Everything else would have seemed like nothing after that. . . . I thought that if maybe I was more loving, I could show him what it is that I wanted. . . . He didn't want me to like hug him or anything like that. If I'd come up behind him to hug him when he was reading the paper or something, he would say, "Are you going to do that long?" Or if he was watching TV and was laying down on the floor, I would come over behind him and just hug him or something and he would just ask me to stop. (Angela)

Martha, who stayed married more than twenty years, vividly described this situation of being invited to come toward her husband and then being rejected when she did reach out to him.

A few years ago, he kept going on and on about what do you want to do for vacation. I finally said to him, "You know what I really want to do?" He said, "No, that's why I'm asking." I said, "I want to go to [a lake south of where they live] on a house boat." . . . He says, "Fine, who with?" I said, "Nobody, just us." He jumped up and slammed his fist on the table and said, "You've got to be crazy if you think I'm going for a week with you." It's just like your insides freeze up. But he got up and walked out. I couldn't say anything more if I wanted to.

The third characteristic in double-bind relationships is that the subject of the abuse cannot comment on the conflicting messages (Bateson 1972). The psychologically abused wife is blocked from commenting in two ways. First, women are taught to repress or deny their anger (Bernstein 1993), which then is projected onto men, which in turn supports the husband's position of power. When this repressed hostility begins to come into awareness, the woman feels anxious. (Chang and James 1987). The second reason for not commenting is her fear of his aggression (Chodorow 1989; Novey and Novey 1983), which she believes will be expressed in further criticism and verbal attack. Two women depicted their versions of this pattern.

I never stood up to him. . . . I thought, I am not going to argue with him. I mean, that was the point our relationship had gotten to. As long as I never questioned him about anything he said or did, everything was fine. As long as I never rocked the boat. (Jeannie)

He would start looking at me like I was gross. He would look at me and just "Ooh." He would say, "Ooh," like, get away from me. He never used to say things like that 'til we got to [city in the south]. He got more verbal then when he would get angry. He would let people know. He always did, but he was louder about it and more verbal. He would say more once we got down there. And I thought, my gosh, if I upset him enough, he's just going to kill me. He's going to kill the kids, he's going to. I wondered if he would. Especially once we got down there. He just scared me down there. I had never been afraid of him before that. (Amy)

The final ingredient in double-bind relationships is a prohibition from escape (Bateson 1972). In psychologically abusive relationships, he tells her that she can't make it without him and that no one else would want her. As long as she believes him, she is trapped.

Looking back, I don't know why I didn't leave him when I was out on my own, supporting myself. You know, all I can think of is that he just had me so browbeaten that I thought, "Well, I guess I'm lucky that I'm married." I still just felt like he was right and I was wrong. (Laura)

He just had so much control over me that he had me convinced that I wasn't going to be able to get a divorce, that I wasn't going to be able to have a life of my own, and that if I did get a divorce, you know, I could not handle anything. I did nothing without [ex-husband's] direction, nothing. I did it exactly the way he wanted me to. (Carol)

Just the fact that he would say, I didn't know how to do anything on my own. That's another reason I was scared to leave was because I didn't think I could do it. . . . I had never done that. I went straight from my house to being married to him. I never lived by myself in-between. (Angela)

Then [ex-husband] proceeded to pack his things and start to leave. It just switched all of the thinking process, so then that made me panicky somehow. I wanted him to stay and I don't remember why I was panicky. Whether it was because I felt like I couldn't put the ends together. He had always said that I was—one of the big things in our life was that [ex-husband] was a college graduate and I was not—dumber than "hell-shit." He always played that up to me. (Vicky)

In a double-bind relationship, the wife is always off balance. Whichever way she goes, she can be criticized. Rather than developing a clear sense of self as a competent adult woman, she feels confused and unsure of herself.

PATTERN THREE: DIRECT VERBAL ATTACKS

The third interaction pattern is direct attacks on the person's worth or verbal attacks (Engels 1990; Forward 1986; Hoffman 1984; Tolman 1989). The husband uses verbal attacks to keep her in her place or to punish her for doing something he didn't approve of. Since she is afraid of his anger and feels forbidden to express her anger (or afraid that if she does he will escalate even more), they develop a pattern in which he verbally attacks her and she either remains silent or tries to defend herself, usually giving up quickly. As Martha said, "He could just say the nastiest, nastiest put-down things."

The dinner table was usually his time to criticize me and to beat me down. It was his opportunity to let the kids know really how I was and what kind of a person I was. . . . I'm too stupid to go to school. They would never accept me in school. He criticized the cooking of the food. He'd criticize how I handled something. (Carol)

He'd wake up and say what a pit the house was, that I never cleaned the house and he had to do it all, and he wasn't doing anything. It just kept going like that no matter what I did. (Rebecca)

He always took every opportunity to put me down. If I dressed up nice, he commented on how much make-up I was wearing. I could never do anything right. (Angela)

It was just little things to begin with, and as time goes on, it gets worse and worse. It was just the idea that your opinion didn't count. In fact, you weren't even allowed to have an opinion. If it didn't agree with his, you were stupid, wrong, dumb, you know. You were never supposed to want to go out, do anything. You were just supposed to take care of the house and kids and be there whenever he got home. Dinner on the table whenever he came home. (Martha)

PATTERN FOUR: SILENCE AND WITHDRAWAL

The fourth pattern in psychological abuse is passive emotional withdrawal. Silence, withdrawal, or unexpressiveness is used as a control tactic in psychologically abusive relationships (Tolman 1992). Being unwilling to talk says a great deal, including who establishes the rules about when and what can be contested or fought about. Generally, this unexpressiveness is an intentional manipulation used when he thinks his position is threatened (Sattel 1983). Betty knew that her husband was mad at her even if he was not yelling at her because he would stop talking to her. Vicki told me that during one period she and her husband hardly spoke to each other for two years. Other women recalled "silent treatments," when their husbands would not talk to them for days.

Every Saturday and every Sunday, it was ten to twelve hours in front of the TV set. So I can't say he was badgering me all the time, 'cause most of the time it was as if I didn't exist. (Martha)

And if he didn't show anger, then [ex-husband] just didn't speak to me. He wouldn't touch me. He could go for days and days without saying anything to me. If I would ask him a question about dinner, he would not even acknowledge that I had asked a question. I really never knew where I stood with him. (Carol)

Having been in relationships that were physically abusive, Tammi was able to compare the effects of withdrawal to other types of abuse.

I was used to the other type of abuse, the verbal, physical, you know, all of that; but then the other kind, I feel like, even to this day, that it's the worst kind 'cause you don't know why this withdrawal is happening. And, I don't even know if they know they are doing it themselves. I really don't even know if they know that. I think they kind of know that they are punishing you, but I don't think they know why they picked to punish you, so it's a withdrawal of communication, a withdrawal of affection, or a withdrawal that you even exist.

You are not there, which is, to me, what I felt like when I was a child. I don't matter, I don't exist. I keep wanting to know, well, what's wrong? I'd ask him, "What's wrong?" and he'd say, "Nothing." But, of course, you know something is because of how he's not really there with you. His body is there, but he's not there. He is not there.

You feel like you're alone. You've done something, but you don't know what you've done because he won't tell you what you've done. . . . I just kept trying to figure out what was wrong. It must have been something I did. What can I do to fix it?

PATTERN FIVE: LACK OF EMOTIONAL CONNECTION

Psychologically abusive relationships are characterized by either criticism and attack or by withdrawal; but the pain the women report comes from more than the demands, the controlling behavior, the verbal battering, and the silent withdrawal. The last pattern involves the wife reaching out for empathy, understanding, or emotional support and the husband responding with anger or withdrawal. The women told of feeling unable to emotionally connect with their spouse. They experienced that their husbands were not really present. As one person said, "He was there, but he wasn't really there." There was almost no sense of being understood, no emotional bond, no belief that they (the women) were valued, and little, if any, warmth or support to balance the harshness.

The concept of emotional intersubjectivity is useful in understanding the lack of emotional connection that exists in psychologically abusive relationships. Denzin (1984) defines emotional intersubjectivity as

the interactional appropriation of another's emotionality such that one feels one's way into the feelings and intentional feeling states of the other. Emotional intersubjectivity is an interactional process that joins two or more persons into a common, or shared, emotional field of experience. (130)

This process allows partners to understand each other's reality and experience. When a person is unwilling to engage in emotional intersubjectivity, "one-sided, empty, spurious emotional understanding may be produced" (Denzin 1984, 138). Many men—with their focus on rational, linear, cognitive understanding—expect women to take care of emotional understanding.

In psychologically abusive marriages, the women put considerable effort into trying to reach emotional understanding of their partner, but this understanding was one-sided. Their husbands seemed to lack the willingness or ability to empathize, or they became impatient or angry when feelings were expressed. One woman's explanation was typical: "My feelings didn't count; if I cried, that was it, he left. I was allowed to be happy, but I wasn't allowed to be sad, or upset, or cry." Their husbands did not seem to know how to respond appropriately to emotional pain or to connect with another person's experience. Jeannie revealed, "Whenever I let my emotions show, he made light of them. He couldn't accept them and I felt hurt, so I started hiding my feelings by eating. When I felt bad, I ate."

Laura was in a serious car accident; she hit another car and it rolled over. When she got home, she went to the bedroom and cried.

I was an absolute emotional wreck because I couldn't believe that I hurt someone or caused an accident so severe. I didn't know what the extent of her injuries were. A while later he [her husband] came in and asked me something about dinner. I made some comment about I didn't ever want to drive again and he just started yelling at me. He told me I needed to snap out of it. . . . He just wasn't sympathetic at all. Anyway, it was at that moment in time that I felt like I can never depend on him for emotional support.

When an aunt that Angela had been very close to as a child died, she started to cry; he came upstairs and asked,

"What happened?" I said, "My aunt died." He said, "Well, it wasn't like she wasn't sick or anything" and he left. That just made me cry even more.

Even in a crisis, such as illness, the spouse was not supportive or empathic. When Carol was rushed to the emergency room, she became very upset knowing that her husband would be furious with her if she was hospitalized and not around to take care of his needs. After the doctor told her she would have to be in the hospital seven to nine days, her husband walked out the door.

He didn't say good-bye to me or the doctor or anybody. When he left, the doctor told me, "There are some serious problems between you and your husband." I said, "No, there isn't." He said, "Yes there is. You nearly died three times and your husband has not expressed any concern whatsoever."

Other women talked about their husbands' unwillingness to respond to any of the women's physical problems. Kathy, who had some serious health problems, said, "He's very nonsupportive of illness." Other women reported that their husbands were around even less than usual when they were pregnant or sick.

When I would get like a stomachache or a headache, I would say, "God, my stomach hurts," or "My head hurts." He would just throw a fit. I could never tell him that I had anything wrong with me. I broke my toe last summer. I told him and he said, "Oh great, this is just going to cost me more money." I said, "Well, can I just go to the doctor? I have to have something done about it. My whole foot is swollen." He said, "No, you may not. I don't have the money to send you to a doctor." [This couple had a middle-class income.] (Amy)

I was so sick I couldn't stand up without leaning up against the wall, I felt that bad. And he'd be like, "Oh, just go on back to bed." He couldn't handle it at all. (Jeannie)

Becky remembered this conversation taking place before her daughter was born.

I said, "I know you go boating, but I think this baby's going to be here soon. Could you please stay home with me today?" "Oh, goddamn, stay home. You think you're going to have this kid today, do you? Do you think you're the only goddamn woman that ever had a baby?" I said, "Hey, asshole, it's the first time I ever had a baby. What about me?" "Oh, there you go again, what about me, what about me." I said, "Go on the boat, I don't care what you do, I'll have a neighbor take me to the hospital. Forget it, just go. I don't want you here if that's how you feel."

Talking about the lack of emotional connection between herself and her husband, Jeannie felt, "He wasn't really there and he didn't care." This sense that he was not really present, that he was not emotionally available was repeated in each woman's story.

He was not affectionate. He was never very affectionate, but [at first] at least I could feel the love and I could feel him there. I just didn't feel him there anymore. I felt I was doing everything myself, everything I needed done. He wouldn't help me do anything. . . . I would do things for him, but he wouldn't do anything for me. . . . I didn't have the one thing that I wanted and that was him. He was there, but he wasn't really there. (Angela)

There was no underlying sense of warmth, only a fantasy that love and caring could be available if only she could meet his demands. But, as Dorothy affirmed, that is impossible. Once she got one area about the way he wanted it, he would change his expectations or, as she put it, "The goalposts would be lifted up and moved down the field" and he would still be dissatisfied. Other women recounted the same process. Jeannie was always told that "if only you lose weight" then everything would be okay, but when she lost weight he was mad at her about something else. As soon as the woman met one expectation, another flaw would be identified and a new expectation created.

This fantasy that "everything will be okay if" is particularly tantalizing, because with other people these men often seem charming and giving. The wife sees him giving other people what she wants. When Carol was seriously sick and in the hospital, her husband never came to see her. But when one of the men that worked for her husband was hospitalized, her husband went to visit him every day and called the man's wife every night to see if she needed anything.

Martha's husband also paid attention to other people and not her.

We started going to dances years ago with a big group of people. There might be ten or twelve women in the group. He had to dance with every one of them. When I wanted to dance, he was too tired or his back hurt.

I was trying to explain to him how I felt about those dances, and he just instantly hit the ceiling. He says, "I don't give a goddamn about your feelings and emotions. Other people are more important."
It was the idea of always impressing other people. His family was always last on the totem pole. It wasn't just me, it was the kids or anything. It was impressing people or it was sports that always came first in his life. He was always doing these things for other people just so they'd think how great he was, but then he'd never stop and think what he was doing to his family and what his family thought of him.

Veronica also described this phenomenon: "This man who has a gift of gab, who could talk about everything and anything, never talked to me." Angela revealed that many times she watched him give other people the attention that she wanted.

When we were in Boston, he had a friend over there at work. I suspected that was the reason things were going bad then. He got really close to her when we separated, talking on the phone. . . . He talks to all these women, but he doesn't talk to me. So all the problems he had he was bringing to her and not to me.

In each of the five interaction patterns common in psychologically abusive marriages, the husband maintains a dominating position, functioning more like a parent or controlling boss. He acts against his wife, who becomes object. Each of these psychologically abusive interaction patterns are experienced as creating a sense of hopelessness and despair. Her increasingly submissive and adaptive position results in a gradual loss of sense of self as separate and unique. In the next chapters, we will watch how psychologically abusive relationships evolve from the idealistic hopes at the time of the marriage to despair.

6

BECOMING HIS WIFE

I kept trying to heal our marriage. I wanted to change it, to make it better. I kept looking for things to make it better. (63-year-old self-employed woman)

I didn't think I could do anything right. I tried and I tried and I tried. I kept trying harder and harder and harder. I tried to keep the house cleaner. I tried to keep the kids quiet. He would bring things home and he didn't want the kids to make noise. They weren't allowed to chew gum. They weren't allowed to make noise. I ran around trying to keep small children from making noise, which is impossible, and it drove me crazy. He would just get so angry. (37-year-old woman who was not employed during her marriage)

In the previous chapters, we have looked at psychological abuse from several perspectives: descriptive characteristics, interactional patterns, and cultural/societal influences. Each of these perspectives is important to a complete understanding of psychological abuse. In this chapter, we will look at psychological abuse as an evolving process involving shifts in both partners and in the relationship. Using the women's narratives, we will hear the answers to two core questions: How did their view of the relationship, of their husbands, and of themselves change over time? And what factors influenced the shifts?

In our patriarchal society, women learn that men are the ones "presumed to know," so his definition of reality must be accurate. They also learn that women are responsible for other people's happiness. If their husband is not happy, it must be their fault. As long as a woman's story is constructed using a patriarchal model, his assertion that the relationship is fine and she is flawed is accepted, and his abusive behavior is considered an understandable response given her less-than-perfect behavior as a wife. His abuse is experienced as caused by her limitations. She adapts her behavior in an attempt to satisfy his demands and hopefully to please him. The interpretative theory guiding her behavior and her understanding of her reality is traditional gender positioning learned first from her mother and reinforced by society. At this point, individual agency is very limited, and social structural forces dominate. Social norms and deeply embedded expectations about what women and wives are supposed to do govern her behavior.

Although in retrospect some women identified that the man's need for control and dominance was evident during the courtship, these women's relationship stories generally began positively. Often the patterns of domination were seen by the women as indications of strength. In most cases, the abusive behavior did not start until the relationship faced the first challenge, generally the wife's becoming pregnant. With her pregnancy, she had less energy for him and began to turn inward. He experienced this as an unacceptable shift of attention. The abuse became more problematic with the birth of the first child, at which time the husband was no longer the center of his wife's universe.

After the abuse begins, the relationship follows a predictable pattern. The stages in this process may overlap and vary in length of time, but the process is similar from one situation to another. In the early period, the wife believes that any problems the relationship has must be her fault and thinks that she can make her husband happy. In the middle phases, her perception begins to change, and she is aware of the serious emotional and physical consequences of living in an abusive relationship. In the final stage, she begins to turn to herself for satisfaction and to withdraw from her husband. In this chapter, the early phases of the relationship will be discussed.

IF ONLY I TRY HARDER

In the beginning, there is generally an extended period of time during which the wife denies the relationship problems and believes that "if only" she makes some change then everything will be okay. Blaming herself for his angry abusive behavior, the wife believes that everything will be okay if only she does what he wants her to do, if only she is a more perfect wife. For many of the participants, this system of believing that she could get recognition if only she could do or be more began in childhood.

As she grew up, this belief that a change in her behavior would change the feeling state in another person was maintained. She learned that part of being a good wife is keeping her husband happy and if he is not happy she should change. She keeps believing that if only she can be a better wife then he will be happy and will give her recognition and treat her with consideration.

The metamorphosis of a woman into a wife involves a redefinition of the self and an active reshaping of her personality to conform to the wishes, needs, and demands of her husband. She holds no real power, makes more concessions and adjustments than her husband, and is often reconciled, not happy. (Goodrich et al. 1988, 49)

Women often hold themselves exclusively accountable for the success or failure of the relationship. Any perceivable improvements in the relationship must mean that her efforts are working and that the goal of a positive relationship is achievable. "By finding things to alter in herself, she at once undermines herself, protects herself, and keeps herself hopeful" (Burstow 1992, 152). She undermines herself by constantly blaming and criticizing herself; she protects herself from having to face the hurtful aspects of her relationship with her husband and, believing that as soon as she improves enough the relationship will be fine, she can be hopeful.

All the women talked about their belief that if only they could be a better wife then their husbands would stop the abusive behavior.

I thought that if I could be more perfect then it would work. I went to church on Sundays. I am a Christian and I felt like if I was Christian enough then it would work. I felt like it was all my problem. The reason he reacted this way to me was because of me. I had to do something that would get his attention, that would straighten things out. I had to straighten things out myself. Just like when I was a kid. I was the one that had to straighten it all out because it rested on me. (Carol)

He became verbally abusive, becoming upset if I needed a pair of hose more often than he thought I needed them. He became jealous of men at work and my job was never as good or demanding as his. He de-graded my profession and my coworkers. It was easier to quit to make him happy. It was okay as long as I conformed to the way he wanted things done. (Jeannie)

Anytime I did anything he didn't like, it was always I wasn't putting him first. . . . He told me that all the time. So I thought, well, if I want to make him happy, that's what I've got to do. But I was never his priority. He was his priority. (Laura)

Looking at this process of trying to improve, to be perfect, Coward (1984) explains that the dissatisfaction women experi-ence is "recast as desire . . . for something more, . . . displaced into desire for the ideal" (13). Women are offered the promise of future perfection and pleasure "if only" they lose weight and look lovely, are wonderful cooks, have a clean house, and/or have perfectly behaved, quiet children. When you achieve these ideals you'll feel better, just try harder or try another method. While focusing on achieving some impossible ideal that exists only as the end product of photographic techniques, women avoid facing the pains and gaps in their relationships with their husbands and seeing the inequality built into our patriarchal so-ciety.

His abusive behavior is labeled as acceptable, an understand-able response given her less-than-perfect behavior as a wife. She knows that she is not a perfect housekeeper, does not have a model figure, is not a constantly attentive wife; therefore, she assumes that he has a right to be critical. She apologizes and promises to improve. Having learned that they are responsible for other people's happiness, women adapt their behavior hoping to satisfy their husbands' demands and make them happy.

This attempt to change, to be a perfect wife so that the marriage will improve, was reported by all the participants. They believed that it was possible to change the relationship by changing their behavior, the way they looked, the way their children acted. Although their behavior was driven by unrealistic goals, there was evident a quality of individual agency and belief in self as they pushed themselves to be perfect.

I tried to make things better by being the perfect wife. I'd have dinner ready and everything cleaned up. He expected me to vacuum every day. He'd look for the lines that the vacuum leaves on the carpet. (Amy)

I think I was trying to make it change. If I did this, he wouldn't drink as much. If I kept [their daughter] away from him, he wouldn't lose his temper. If the house was cleaner, he'd be happy. I really did all those things. I took a lot more effort with the house. He was working nights at the time and I'd put [their daughter] to bed like at 8:00 and I'd work on the house until 11:00 when I woke him up to get ready for work. (Rebecca)

I've tried my damnedest, you know. We know none of us are perfect. I mean we all have faults and yet when you've tried and tried and tried, and you get nowhere, what else can you do?

I let him get by with doing it. See, he even told his daughter, . . . "Nobody ever said no to me. Everybody lets me get my way." But myself plus the kids, as they got older, would try to talk back to him, reason to him, and he'd just knock 'em down with words, not physically. (Martha)

[Ex-husband's] image to the world is very important, and his job and how he looks to other people is extremely important. When things started getting really bad, we were still going to church. We were still teaching Sunday school. Him and I both taught . . . our class about personality differences and relationships and marital problems and problems with your children. I asked him so many times, "Why couldn't we apply some of this to our lives?" He said, "There is nothing wrong with the way we do things." It just amazed me because [ex-husband] is extremely intelligent, but he could not see what was going on. (Carol)

As long as she accepts his definition that there is nothing wrong with the relationship and the only problems are flaws in her, she thinks that she must continue to try to change. Although they tried and tried, it was never enough. They became exhausted with the effort.

I tried in vain to make him happy because I just knew if he was happy then things would be all right. Nothing I did or said ever made him happy. I was worn to a frazzle! . . . Even as my physical and emotional health was failing and I was finding it hard to get by day to day, I still kept trying to do just the thing that would save us all and fix this mess. Even though I became hospitalized, like a drowning victim coming to the surface for the last breath of air, I tried in vain even as I went down to do the right thing to save us and fix the whole mess. (Carol)

NEVER GOOD ENOUGH

Thinking that a relationship with a man is necessary for their survival, many women are vulnerable to intimidation and abuse. Having learned to define themselves by their relationships, they lose all sense of identity without a relationship (Bernstein 1993). Furthermore, women often give their roles as wife and mother priority and highly value succeeding in these roles (Ferraro and Johnson 1983). The woman and her partner know that to be a good wife and mother she must put everyone else's needs ahead of hers. Virginia Woolf (1970) named this image of how wives are supposed to act the "Angel in the House": She is always sympathetic, charming, and unselfish. Today, women still learn that they should be self-effacing, restrained, nice, or "Angels in the House." They must try to satisfy their husbands and keep them happy, but often this is impossible. "Never quite good enough or quick enough, she regularly encounters his haranguing temper and judges herself as a just target for his rage and disdain" (Goodrich et al. 1988, 169).

The women in the study discussed their beliefs that they should be able to keep their husbands happy. The need to keep him happy was a driving force even though they were never able to succeed.

I tried to be a chameleon, to blend into everything, to make him happy so that he's not upset. If he's upset then he's going to drink and think it's my fault. He's telling me, "I'm drinking because I'm very unhappy and I'm unhappy because of the way you're acting." You know, he thinks that I always treated him like shit. That was his deal and I look back now and I think, I mean this was a man that I just did everything that I was requested to do. And I treated him like shit? This was a man that probably mowed the grass twenty times out of seventeen years. This was a man that never offered. (Debbi)

No matter how hard I tried to please him it was never enough. But I kept trying. I had this instilled in me that you had to do whatever it took to make a marriage work. And that was one thing my mother told me the night I left to get married. My mother told me that it was my responsibility to do whatever it took to make him happy and I believed that for a long time. She gave me some very bad advice. (Jeannie)

The women continued to offer recognition, support, and caring even though they were not receiving positive recognition from him.

It's a twist. He's the one who has been unfaithful to me. He's the one who has had various affairs. He's the one who has done various things, but I'm always having to prove that I am faithful, that I love him, that I'm there. Where it should be that I need the affirmation from him, but I'm always giving him the affirmations. (Betty)

All of these women had children. They were constantly torn between the demands of their husbands and the needs of their children.

One of the things he said to me was, "You were with the children too much. I felt neglected." And I said to him, "If you had done some of these things, if you had worked with [one daughter] on her multiplication tables, if you had helped [the other daughter] on her Science Fair project, hey, you know, I wouldn't have had to. I would have been there for you." (Kathy)

We would have plans and he would need to be in control of the situation. . . . Anytime I did anything he didn't like, it was always I wasn't putting him first. (Laura)

The women doubted themselves because they were not able to keep their husbands happy. These doubts made them more vulnerable to believing the attacks were true. Many of them thought they probably deserved to be abused and probably had no better option. Continued abuse further increased the abuser's control as the criticism, attacks, insults, and accusations destroyed her self-esteem and confidence, leaving her unable to judge the relationship realistically.

I BELIEVED HIM

Women in psychologically abusive relationships accept that their husbands' view of reality is correct. They think the problems are their fault, stemming from their inadequacies (Forward 1986; Goodrich, et al. 1988). They agree with their husbands that the fact that they see the world differently means that there is something wrong with them. This thought that there is something wrong with them contributes to their belief "that they lack the capacity to be autonomous" (Bartky 1990, 30), so they must stay in the relationship.

Lacan's (1977) ideas about interpretation are helpful in understanding this phenomenon. Interpretation is the process in which one person defines reality or explains reality to another person. The interpreter has the power or, as Lacan would say, is the "subject presumed to know." The husband identifies what is true, what is important, what has meaning in all of reality including what is true about her: how she feels, what she thinks, and what she wants.

This hold he had on me. He was so persuasive. He could manipulate me in any way. If I said, "I'm unhappy," he'd say, "No, you're not." And he would make me believe I was not unhappy. He would spend hours making me believe I was not unhappy. I mean he would sit down with me until 3:00 in the morning many times, explaining to me why he was right and I was wrong. (Amy)

I kept thinking if I would do something right that he would appreciate it, but nothing I did was ever right. Even to this day, it's like it was really hard for me to admit that there was abuse because he stood there and told me that there wasn't and I believed him. Everything he ever told me I believed. (Carol)

He would immediately start saying what I was feeling was wrong. After eight or nine years of marriage, I asked him, "Why should I communicate with you, because you always tell me I'm wrong?" (Laura)

He never thought he was doing anything wrong. He never admitted that it was anything he was doing. When I did try to talk to him, he wouldn't listen and he'd tell me what I should be thinking and feeling, what he thought. He wouldn't listen to what I was saying, so in essence I think I did shut down. (Rebecca)

As the emotional abuse continues, the woman believes it must be true, she probably deserves to be abused and probably has no better option. Older women have stayed in this early phase of the relationship for years. With little permission to leave the marriage and great fears, they do not allow themselves to see the extent of the problems. Younger women who have grown up in a time of more options for women move through this phase more rapidly. For women of all ages, the move from following our society's patterns for a wife to a different view of a woman's role in a relationship is a challenge. In the next chapter, we will focus on the turning points that occur as women change their views of their relationships.

7

TURNING POINTS

It is on the day that we can conceive of a different state of affairs that a new light falls on our troubles . . . and we decide that these are unbearable.

—Jean-Paul Sartre (1966, 411)

I could not let myself go back to all that mental/verbal abuse. Now weight was not the issue. It was money, sex, the kids, the house, etc., etc. I finally saw it was anything I did. I was wrong. I was never going to get what I needed from this man. (43-year-old woman)

This process of trying to make the relationship work sometimes lasts years before the woman begins to modify the meanings she gives to her experience. She cannot change until she reconstructs her narrative, giving up her belief that he is the one who can define reality and that all relationship problems are her fault. Eventually she must change her view of herself, of her spouse, and of their relationship, as well as change her thoughts about what she can do.

During this middle period of the relationship, she begins to doubt her ability to satisfy him, she wonders whether he does love her, and she begins to doubt his position that the problems are all her fault. There is a major shift from thinking it is all her fault to wondering about him. She begins to shift from seeing him as Mr. Wonderful, her savior, to viewing him as abusive; from seeing herself as his caretaker to realizing that she is unable to please him; and from believing she cannot make it without him to realizing she might have to leave him. Gradually, she begins to move from being the guilty one to being the victim and then to being the capable person. There is also a change in her narrative of the future: the story becomes projective rather than recollective. This projection must shift to a story that shows life as being better without him.

There is a major shift in perception from blaming herself to looking critically at him. She is no longer sure that he would be loving "if only" she made some change. By now she has tried so many times to satisfy him that she begins to question whether he can be satisfied. As Dorothy explained, he kept moving the goalpost so no matter what she did he was not satisfied. Jeannie said, "I finally realized that no matter what I did, it wouldn't make him happy." In every case, her emerging awareness that there was nothing she could do that would affect his basically constant dissatisfaction was a critical factor in her ability to change her view of herself, her husband, and the relationship.

In the beginning of this process, she asks herself where she stands with him. Carol related,

I'd ask him on many occasions to hit me 'cause at least I'd know where I stood. I didn't even know whether he even cared about me at all and he wouldn't even really comment. He would stare at me like I was crazy.

Thinking it would be easier if their husband would hit them was mentioned by a number of participants. Physical abuse was viewed as a solid, understandable communication. If he hits me, that means he does not love me. If he criticizes and verbally attacks me—saying it is for my own good in order to help me become a better wife so he can love me—that must mean he does love me. She believes there must be something wrong with her after all; he does not think they have any problems and he does not hit her.

Gradually she begins to question the meaning of his communication, to doubt his definition of reality. With this shift from blaming herself to seriously wondering about him, she begins to believe that maybe it isn't all her fault. She begins to sees that no matter what she does he is not going to be satisfied. One forty-three-year-old woman explained, "I finally saw it wasn't anything I did. I was wrong. I was never going to get what I needed from this man."

The other women also discussed this change in their views of their husbands and their expectations for their marriages.

I decided to go to school after a really nasty night of having to perform sexually. . . . I don't remember a lot, but I can remember waking up the next day and thinking . . . love's not supposed to hurt. Something is not right here. So if I can't do well, or if I can't do good enough here, by gosh I'm going to go to school and maybe I can do good there. (Dorothy)

No matter what I say, it's not going to make any difference. I just listen and then sometimes I wish he would get over this so we could get on to something else. You know, I just listen. It doesn't do any good to say anything to him.

He cannot give back, he has to keep taking in and if you don't give it to him, then. . . . You know, it's sad, it's real sad. It's sad for him; but, you know, I just don't feel responsible anymore. (Betty)

You got to the point you didn't expect anymore. You knew it wasn't going to be any different so you didn't expect anything. (Martha)

Sometimes he acts in a way that is inappropriate enough that she cannot continue to deny that he has problems and that the relationship has serious problems. After an incident when her husband got drunk and left their young child alone, Rebecca made a major shift.

I didn't trust him. I adored him until that point. After that it was hard to even be near him. . . . After it started really falling apart, then I had a more objective look at it and reasoned that it really wasn't my fault . . . . It was kind of like the rose-colored glasses came off—shattered. I saw what it was really like and had been and what was in the future. (Rebecca)

This shift from seeing him as the authority, the one "presumed to know," the definer of reality, is facilitated by the continuous nature of psychological abuse. There are no breaks when he is remorseful and the relationship is positive. The women in this study reported that the pattern of remorse so common in physically abusive relationships is almost nonexistent in psychologically abusive relationships. With remorse, the husband admits that his physically abusive behavior was wrong and begs for forgiveness, promising to never hurt her again. Psychologically abusing husbands do not seem to see their behavior as inappropriate, so there is nothing to be sorry about. There are few periods of solicitude and hope that everything will be fine that are so common in physically abusive relationships. Psychologically abusive husbands identify their behavior as correct and justified. The abuse is ongoing.

For all the women, this stage of the relationship involved them developing an alternative definition of their relationship. Rather than believing their husbands' definition of reality, which was "we do not have any problems, it is you that has the problems," they began to create an alternative view that identified that their relationships had problems. They began to believe "we do have problems, but maybe we can fix them."

COUNSELING: THE SHIFT FROM PRIVATE TO PUBLIC

For many of the women, this new explanation of their situation led to the decision to seek counseling. This constituted a major turning point. The woman had to go against society's rules about making private troubles public and take her problems into the public arena, to a public institution "created to address those personal problems" (Denzin 1989a, 10). This shift from private to public was done out of desperation about the pain in the relationship and the continued hope that it was possible to save the relationship. Their husbands were resistant and many refused counseling. Those who agreed to try counseling did not continue beyond a few sessions. The men seemed to have no motivation to change themselves and went for a variety of other reasons.

He said, "I'm going to see what she's going to say about me. I want to defend myself." That was his whole reason for going. It was never a matter of going to try to make the marriage better. (Martha)

A few of the men went to counseling but quit because they thought the therapists were siding with their wives.

So he decided that he's going to stop seeing [their counselor] 'cause, "You know he's on your side. He's not on my side." (Veronica)

We went to counseling, but he would stop going any time an issue came up that he couldn't deal with or something where [their counselor] thought I was right. (Jeannie)

Finding fault with the therapist was a common excuse for giving up on counseling.

I asked him to go into counseling and we attended some counseling. His remarks to that was, "Well, it's not [specific religion] counseling." And so therefore he didn't feel that he could get anything out of it because these people didn't understand [specific religion] values and therefore they couldn't counsel us about our marriage. So we went for a short time and his resistance says that it wasn't going to work and the counselor realized that and so we just withdrew from that. (Tamika)

Often the husband's agenda was to get the counselor to side with him and tell his wife what was wrong with her.

[Ex-husband] made a comment to me when we had an appointment with this counselor, he said, "I can't wait to get you in to see that marriage counselor so he can see how you are. So the world, you know, is going to know what a lousy wife you are." And so I was basically expecting this counselor to come down hard on me. (Laura)

If the therapist did not blame the wife, the husband might criticize and blame her in front of the counselor.

He picked the counselor and then he proceeded to tell me what I couldn't talk about to the counselor. And I went in there and talked about it and he got really angry that he had to admit to somebody, "Yes, he had gone to a massage parlor." That really made him very angry.

He admitted it. "Yeah, I did, like, so what, she made me." That was it. "She made me drink." I made him do that, I made him seek other women for companions. I guess that really probably was the turning point, but yet again it made me realize what really went on, that I couldn't trust him. But, I still carried on a relationship. I still wanted to put the marriage back together. (Debbi)

I went to see a marriage counselor. He [ex-husband] said it was all my fault. If I had kept the house cleaner or been home more, things would have been okay. He didn't admit that he had a drinking problem. He called me "lazy." . . . He would say, "No, it was my problem and he'd go for me, but he wouldn't go for us." (Rebecca)

More frequently the men maintained their public persona in front of the therapist and verbally attacked their wives on the trip home.

He went twice when I was in counseling at church. He stopped going after that because I said something to the counselor. He would not have anything to say at all in the counseling session even when she specifically asked him a question. He said he was just there to get me through whatever I was dealing with. He didn't want to talk about anything. He didn't have anything bothering him. But as soon as we got in the car, all the way home he would yell at me and scream at me about how stupid I am, how I don't even know what I'm talking about, there's nothing going on in our relationship, that I'm talking about things that aren't really happening. He was thinking that I went in there and told that woman a bunch of lies. So the second time he went with me, I said to her up front, I told her I could not talk about things because I said, "As soon as we get in the car, he's going to yell at me." He was furious because I even told her that.

I finally stopped going to counseling because it just made things worse. He neglected me even more. He spoke to me very little. I just decided that I couldn't deal with it. What I did have was better than what I wasn't going to have if I didn't leave things alone, so I just decided to drop out of counseling. (Carol)

TRAPPED

At this point in the relationship, the abused woman knew that a change in her behavior was not going to make her husband stop abusing her, saw the problems in the relationship, and realized that even counseling could not change her husband and their relationship; but still she stayed in the relationship. Why? What had her trapped or stuck in a situation that was destructive to her? Looking at the trap from a societal point of view, patriarchy has defined divorce as bad. In a discussion of physically abused women, Burstow (1992) identified:

Whether she has an analysis of the larger situation or not, and whether she has many illusions or no illusions at all, she stays because she is stuck in a patriarchal society that creates and mystifies the problem of wife abuse and gives only token help to battered women. (152)

In a discussion of why women do not leave physically abusive relationships, Dobash and Dobash (1979) identified cultural proscriptions that also apply to psychologically abusive relationships.

To leave her husband permanently she must overcome not only personal fears, the loss of status, and ambivalent feelings about her husband; but also the deeply ingrained ideas that marriages should be held together at almost any cost, that the split up of a marriage is mostly the fault of the woman, and that a broken home is worse for children than a whole, though violent, one. These cultural notions are urged upon her by friends, relatives, and representatives of social agencies. (147–48)

These same fears and beliefs were discussed by women in psychologically abusive relationships. Personal fears and beliefs that divorce is wrong kept many of the women in these marriages.

I wanted it to work. I loved him. I was brought up that when you get married, you stayed married and that's it. You help each other. I've got a real strong moral, ethical background. You know, twelve years of [private religious schooling] really just puts the screws to you. (Kathy)

The reason I stayed in it so long, besides fear, was that I just didn't want to go through another divorce. (Rebecca)

Another significant reason for staying was the belief that their children needed their father.

I was kind of miserable when the kids were around 10 and 11 years old. We had no intimacy, no love, no tenderness, no sexual encounters, you know, maybe once a month, but that was absolutely feelingless. I just decided that I was going to make a go of it until the kids left the house. I felt like they needed a father and a mother and that was my goal. (Vicky)

I had a roof over my head, food on the table, and a nice car to drive. What else did I want? My decision was to stay in the marriage for the kids, hoping all the time he would change, but he never did. I put all my energy into my kids. I stopped asking him where he'd been, why wouldn't he come home?

We were just tolerating each other the last eight to ten years. Neither of us believe in divorce. I guess the failure is that he couldn't do anything to change and I couldn't do anything more. He just wasn't willing. He wanted everything the way it used to be. (Jeannie)

Some stayed because they still had fantasies that maybe their relationships could be saved.

When I think back over my childhood, there were probably a lot of times when my mom couldn't love my dad. And I guess I saw that he changed. And I thought my husband would too, but he didn't. He wasn't going to. (Jeannie)

Many of the women had the material things they needed and were worried about the financial effects of leaving.

I knew I would have to go back to my mom's and that bothered me. I had all the material things and was just not ready to give all that up. Also I was concerned about taking [her daughter] away from her father. I was just waiting for him to give me a reason. Some kind of something—hit me. I wanted him to hit me so bad. (Amy)

As I went through the therapy groups and more and more of the counseling, I realized that I was in an abusive situation and I need to get out of it, but I was so scared of losing the kids. I thought the only option I had was either being in what I had or going back to what I had, living with my parents because I financially did not have a job. I hadn't worked for years, and [ex-husband] had convinced me that I was too stupid to go to school and I was even too stupid to work. (Carol)

I felt kind of trapped. I didn't want to jerk my daughter out of school. Plus I was making a plan to save up some money to leave to get out. (Becky)

Escalating their power tactics, the abuser may threaten to cause emotional or financial damage to his wife by doing such things as gaining custody of the children, kidnapping the children, harming himself or someone else, or revealing personal secrets (Shepard 1991). The women in this study felt confused and scared. Their husbands told them they should stay and, after all, they were not being physically abused.

He kept telling me I shouldn't leave because he never hit me. I felt guilty. I didn't think I had a reason to leave. I told him he was verbally abusive, but he'd just say he never hit me. I thought about leaving for three years. (Amy)

Another reason that many women stayed is that they rejected any option that might hurt anyone, even their abusing husbands. This continuing belief that she must take care of and protect her abusing husband from pain and loss is also a theme in physically abusive relationships (Burstow 1992). Psychologically abusive husbands do not admit their dependency, and their wives think that their husbands could not manage without them.

Over the years, I'd hate to say how many times, I, in my own mind, have threatened to leave. I really should have, for my children's sake, years and years ago. But I always get to thinking about him. He won't understand why I am leaving. To this day, he does not understand, because it was the poor, little, hurt me [ex-husband]. "I didn't do anything wrong." I got to thinking of his feelings and that he would be so hurt if I left, you know. I felt like a mother deserting a sick child. I think that was the role. I always felt more like the mother than a wife. (Martha)

A central reason these women did not leave the relationships was that they did not think they had another option. Having grown up in a patriarchal society, the women had learned that a woman needs a man, that she cannot make it on her own. Sometimes this childhood belief continues to control the thoughts and feelings of women even when they have alternative, rational information. Instead of gaining confidence in their capacity through their adult years, in many ways the development of psychologically abused women is arrested and their confidence eroded during the marriage. After being beaten down for years and told they could never make it on their own, they feel trapped, like they do not have any other alternative. As Becky realized, "He convinced me. You can't do it, you can't make it, and just on and on and on. I don't know. They just have that way of convincing you and I just felt like such a zero for such a long time."

Early in the relationship the woman believes she can make it all okay by changing herself. Hoping it will get better, she can tolerate the stress. She believes in her own ability to fix the situation. During the middle phase of the relationship, this hope is eroded and her belief that she can make him happy and can solve the relationship is shattered. Now she knows that she is trapped in a relationship that is destroying her. In the next chapter, we will hear about the physical and emotional effects of this desperate situation.

8

PHYSICAL AND
EMOTIONAL REACTIONS

I would go to work to escape and then as soon as I hit the
house, I would sit on the couch and just be so totally depressed. . . . As long as I'm doing something and out there,
I feel a lot better about myself. When I go back to my home
situation, I feel depressed (44-year-old nurse)

Ongoing oppression creates a sense of helplessness and leads to
"behaviors that suggest lack of confidence, ability, or capacity to
effect changes in themselves or in the systems that oppress them"
(Norman and Mancuso 1980, 3). Think about the effect of living
day to day with someone who might criticize you or attack you
at any moment. Think of trying to second guess what he wants
or expects in hopes of avoiding being attacked, but you are never
able to please him, whatever you do isn't good enough or right
enough. Add to this the belief that you can never leave this relationship. What would your response be?

DENIAL

During the early phases of the relationship after the abuse
starts, there is generally an extended period of time during which
the wife denies the seriousness of the problem to herself and
others in order to protect his image to herself and to others. Al-

though the women in the group experienced a lot of pain, they hid the problems, which meant there was no one to validate their experiences and challenge their denial. Listen to how they explain this process.

I always made excuses for him, even though I knew they weren't true. But he was supposed to be this perfect person, so I couldn't think of him as being anything else than that.

I didn't have anyone to talk to. I tried to talk to Mom, but I was also trying to be careful about what I said. I guess I was defending his image. He was charming with other people. (Amy)

I took care of my family and worked. From the outside observer, my life was probably picture perfect. I did a lot of covering up to make it appear so. I was so unhappy. I wasn't sure what to do about it, so I kept busy and tired. I did little for myself. (Dorothy)

As long as I didn't think about the things that he did, it was okay. As long as I didn't complain about him, everything was fine. . . . As long as I didn't think about how unhappy I was, I was fine. (Angela)

These women wanted to believe that their husbands loved them and that the marriage would work. They tried to focus on his good points to avoid thinking about losing the security of being married. Laura felt, "I've got to work on this; he's so wonderful. I don't want to lose him." Only in retrospect could they see that he had little capacity to love.

I wanted to believe that he did love me and that he wouldn't do anything or wouldn't say anything that wasn't true. I realize now that I don't think [ex-husband] ever loved me, 'cause I don't think he's capable of love. (Carol)

My mom would say, "Don't you remember the time when he put you down in front of your friends and you cried and cried and cried?" And I said, "I don't remember that, Mom." Then my girlfriend would say, "Don't you remember the time when you came over here and you were explaining about building your house and everything that you said, he corrected you?" I just think I was so brainwashed or just that was just the way it was supposed to be that it just didn't sink in. (Veronica)

I JUST LOST MYSELF

Psychological abuse is emotional violence. Denzin (1984) defines violence "as the attempt to regain, through the use of emotional or physical force, something that has been lost" (169). Psychologically abusive husbands may sense a loss of love, of control, or of power; but the use of emotional violence only intensifies the loss, since his acts of domination gradually destroy her subjectivity, a sense of self. The more she adapts to him, the more of her unique self is lost to both of them. Describing abusive interaction patterns, Denzin (1984) makes clear that rather than interacting with his partner, the abuser interacts at or against her, transforming her into an object toward which he can inflict his emotions.

Benjamin (1988) explains that "domination begins with the attempt to deny dependence" (52). The man fears engulfment and defends against identification and dependency on his mother and later his wife by being powerful and dominant and by not recognizing her. While this behavior responds to his need for independence, it ultimately destroys her subjectivity, leaving him with no one to recognize him. As he negates and controls his wife, he destroys her unique identity and will; she ceases to exist as a conscious being (Benjamin 1988). The hoped-for connection or intersubjective experience is lost in the subject/object, master/slave relationship (Denzin 1985).

A destructive cycle is established. The more power and domination he uses, the more subjectivity she loses. She becomes less herself and more withdrawn from him. With less of her available, his loss is intensified so he escalates his use of emotional violence; indeed, any relationship that forces adaptation to another person will lead to some loss of sense of self (Benjamin 1988; Denzin 1984; Herman 1992). Women who have experienced ongoing psychological abuse give voice to this process. In their attempt to please him and avoid criticism, they vigilantly censor their actions, adapting until all sense of unique self is lost.

I think basically what happened was that I totally lost myself as a person. I never quit being a good parent. I always handled the kids, so I just lost myself. (Jeannie)

My self-esteem and self-worth and everything just plummeted. I just kept trying to be what he wanted me to be. (Tammi)

I was dying, I had no identity. I didn't know who I was as a person. (Carol)

Instead of being confirmed and supported within their primary relationships, these women are attacked and criticized. Even though she sacrifices autonomy and her unique sense of identity or self as she adapts to her husband's demands and tries to satisfy him, she is unable to create an intimate relationship with him. Her longings for emotional attachment, love, and intimacy and her wish for autonomy or self-realization are thwarted.

DEPRESSION

Many authors (Brown et al. 1986; Gilligan 1982; Jack 1991; Kaplan 1984) identify positive relationships as essential to women's continuing development and sense of well-being. Relationship failures are experienced as their fault and may result in shame, guilt, and depression (Jack 1991). Believing that no matter what she does she cannot achieve the desired outcome of a positive relationship, the woman begins to perceive herself as helpless (Follingstad 1980). In this situation of no options or choices, passivity, learned helplessness, and depression are often the result (Rounsaville 1978; Seligman 1975; Walker 1979).

Major depression has been associated with unhappy marriages (Kiecolt-Glaser et al. 1987; Weissman 1987). In the study that led to this book, the women reported that as the abuse continued they lost their sense of self, became depressed, and often physically sick. Therapists who work with psychologically abused women report that the women's depression is often normalized, that is, the women have been depressed for so long that it seems normal. As one therapist said, "They don't get how sick they are until they are really very, very, sick."

I didn't get angry, I got depressed. (Betty)

It's like I don't have any energy. You know, I think it's because I haven't been able to do anything I wanted for so long, that it's not even important anymore. You know, when you've wanted something for so long and don't have it, then so what? It doesn't make any difference any more. (Martha)

I felt insecure, scared, nervous, depressed. I had very little energy. (Rebecca)

Eating as a way of self-nurturing and a momentary escape from the depression was a response from many women. They got caught in a pattern of eating to soothe their emotional pain and to avoid the emptiness in their lives, but then they were criticized for being overweight.

When I started going to Overeaters Anonymous, I had a lot of suicidal thoughts. I was real unhappy, extremely unhappy. There were times when I came home from work and would sit in front of the TV and eat and watch TV and do nothing. I knew I was depressed, but I couldn't get out of it. I was fine when I was at work. I was very functional when I was at work, but when I came home it was kind of like, what's the sense in living? (Veronica)

I had lost forty pounds at Weight Watchers to fix my marriage. It did not fix my marriage. It didn't make him compliment me or pay any attention to me whatsoever, so I started binging again. I started my compulsive cleaning again and I was to the point where one afternoon I cleaned my toilets seven times. I was crying the whole time because I couldn't stop. (Carol)

When I reached my lowest point, I ate more and grew inside myself. I ate to get the rewards and love I never got from him. I grew more inside myself and totally lost me as a person. I probably stayed there for several years not realizing it. Every time I would try to lose weight and get a good start, I would let him jerk the rug out from under me and I'd go down again. (Jeannie)

PHYSICAL RESPONSES TO PSYCHOLOGICAL ABUSE

When individuals believe that the demands in their life are greater than their ability to cope, a negative emotional and cognitive state of psychological stress is created (Lazarus and Folk-man 1984). Numerous studies have linked stress and an alteration in immune function, which leads to increased suscep-tibility to disease (e.g., Kiecolt-Glaser and Glaser 1991; Cohen, Tyrrell, and Smith 1993). In a controlled study of newlyweds, women in partnerships with high levels of negative or hostile behaviors showed negative immunological changes on four func-tional tests and increases in blood pressure. The negative phys-ical changes were greater for the women than for the men (Kiecolt-Glaser et al. 1993).

Numerous other studies have shown that unhappy marriages are a prime source of stress and that the quality of the relation-ship influences the members' health (Burman and Margolin 1992); Kiecolt-Glaser et al. 1987; Kiecolt-Glaser et al. 1988). Benne (1971) showed that although unhappily married people in her study were economically better off than those who were di-vorced, the unhappily married registered distress on the follow-ing health indexes: "disability, chronic illness, neurosis, depression, and isolation" (348). Ewart et al. (1991) showed a relationship in women between marital dissatisfaction, hostile in-teractions, and increased blood pressure.

The study of the connections, communication, and relation-ships between the mind, the nervous system, and the immune system, psychoneuroimmunology, has demonstrated that "the more habitual the psychological state, the more it inhibits the body" (Kaschak 1992). As psychological abuse becomes more ha-bitual, physical problems become more likely. Physical problems, particularly headaches and gastrointestinal problems, were re-ported by many of the women in this study.

I think the mind can only take so much and then it goes to the body. I think I was physically and mentally exhausted, just coping with every-thing I had to cope with. . . . My body just quit. Although I still am sick, I still get sore throats, I still have to be careful what I do, I'm a whole lot better. I'm better just now since he's gone. (Kathy)

I got really crazy. Emotionally exhausted and even getting sick physi-cally. I was desperate. (Tammi)

I do remember when I moved out, two weeks later, I felt great. I had had a lot of tension right here, a lot of back pain all the time. My husband would always tell me, "You're such a hypochondriac." When I moved out, those pains went away and I know that it had been from the tension that I had from being there. (Angela)

POWER AND ANXIETY

Repression of some parts of the self, which are then projected onto persons of the opposite gender, is part of becoming masculine or feminine. Boys repress feminine qualities, including the wish to nurture and be nurtured, and project these qualities onto women, who eventually have the confusing role of depending on males but at the same time of taking care of them. Girls repress or deny aggression, assertiveness, and the need to be independent and powerful, projecting these qualities onto men (Bernstein 1993).

The wife projects power and authority onto her husband, and he acts it out, enhancing his prestige and minimizing hers. Although some psychologically abused women try to defend their positions against their husbands, most avoid fighting, arguing, and aggression.

I never fought back. I am just not that kind of person. I am scared to fight. I would just go to my room and cry. (Amy)

For the most part, whatever he said basically went. To keep peace, I did it. I didn't like fighting. It was like I had no authority and I think the reason I had no authority in my house was maybe I didn't let myself. (Veronica)

Traditionally, being powerful is seen as unfeminine. Acting in powerful ways may leave women isolated from men and more traditional women. Even acting out of one's own self-interest is experienced by many women as being hurtful, selfish, and aggressive (Miller 1991). Having been taught not to show power directly and not to use their strength in their own behalf to challenge psychological abuse is particularly difficult for women.

From childhood on, women learn to fear abandonment and separation and to believe that they must defer to men to keep from being abandoned (Chernin 1981; Dinnerstein 1976; Orbach

1978). In situations calling for aggression, these women often become anxious (Bernstein 1993). For them, not challenging psychological abuse seems safer than risking separation.

Anxiety occurs when unacceptable thoughts, impulses, feelings, or conflicts begin to come into awareness. "This beginning awareness of unacceptable aspects of self causes a perception of anticipated danger and an experience of anxiety" (Chang and James 1987, 179). Aggressive impulses that were forbidden by parents and other authority figures in childhood (Bernstein 1993) are unacceptable aspects of self for many women. Sullivan stated that anxiety "can be explained plausibly as anticipated unfavorable appraisal of one's current activity by someone whose opinion is significant" (1953, 113). This describes the everyday reality of women in psychologically abusive relationships. Anxiety is also triggered by the tension between needing and loving a person at the same time as one feels hostile toward him (Horney 1937). Again, this is the ongoing reality of psychologically abused women.

I remember I would have anxiety attacks just before he would come home from work because I knew he was going to come home and I'd have to deal with all that. I'd make sure that the kids were cleaned up. Even as the kids got older, I made sure that they were cleaned up and their rooms were cleaned up and everything was in place and the dinner was going and then he didn't always come home. But if he did come home, he'd want his dinner ready and he wanted it cooked perfectly. He didn't accept it if it was overdone because he had been hours late.

I had a constant headache and was very anxious. I was extremely emotional all the time. I cried all the time. I got to the point where I didn't want to go out of the house. (Carol)

This was a real nightmare way to live. I was in terror and fear all the time but kept going. Sometimes I had so much anxiety that I had difficulty doing the most simple things. He made everything worse, reminding me what a mess I was. I was always so tired.

I was depressed, but I was not dysfunctionally depressed. I mean I went on with my day. . . . I functioned, I kept on going, kept on trying to be optimistic. You know, it gets so bad that you don't even know your life is as bad as it is. You know, it becomes, like, so routine, you don't believe that there's anything else.

It was like I was dying. I know that now. I was dying because of my anxiety. It was so bad that my body was breaking down. You know, I have arthritis now really terrible and I'm thirty-eight years old. . . . So I mean, I think you can die from this stuff. (Dorothy)

Following the narrative of women who have been psychologically abused, we find that their first response is to defend with denial, discounting the seriousness or even existence of the problem. They believe his view of reality and blame themselves for not being good enough. Accepting his interpersonal exploitativeness, lack of empathy, narcissistic sense of entitlement, and need to dominate, she ignores her own growing dissatisfaction. Eventually the consistent need to adapt and accommodate to him destroys her sense of self. She becomes less and less of the person she once was and more physically and emotionally ill.

Given the psychological and social pressures these women face, plus years of gender training and adaptation, it is remarkable that any of them are able to move out of psychologically abusive relationships. In the next chapter, we will explore the final turning points that led to a metamorphosis in their lives.

9

COMING OUT

Listen! Listen to what women are saying.
   The "me" I never knew is surging back.
Where I used to feel hollow is where I am deep.
   I was dying. Now I plunge into life.
—Liza Hyatt (1995)

I do like the peace and serenity and if I need to say something to my kids, like I want you to do this, I just say it to them. . . . I think I would rather have the loneliness and peace and serenity, rather than feeling depressed about the way he was treating me. I feel a lot better with him being out of the house. (44-year-old mother of two children)

For most psychologically abused women, giving up hope that the relationship will improve often takes a long time. By the time psychologically abused women finally give up on getting what they want in the relationship, give up on making it okay, give up on the fantasy of living happily ever after, they are exhausted, depressed, and, in many cases, physically sick. Ferraro and Johnson's (1983) discussion of catalysts of change in physically abusive relationships includes loss of hope that the relationship will improve; shreds of hope still linger long after the women have given up intellectually. In a written account of her life, Carol entitled this time as "Later years of marriage: Still struggling, but losing hope." She wrote about the transition in her thoughts about herself.

If I can just do it right, just be the best wife, mother, lover, etc. If I had more faith, if I'm a better Christian, I can do this. I can fix this. I can be perfect. I can make my family happy. I can make everyone love each other. I can! I can! I can! I can't, I can't, I can't! I'm falling, I'm tired, I hurt!

The other women in the study also addressed this process of finally giving up hope.

About one year after I found out about the affair he always denied, I decided to give up. I couldn't make him love me, and I couldn't earn his love, though I tried. (Angela)

I gave up on my marriage three to five years before I made a decision to do something about it. I was tired of trying to make a family when there wasn't one, when I got nothing back from him.
   It's a death. It's worse than somebody dying because it's not really over. You feel like a failure. Something that you wanted to do so badly, you couldn't do. Accepting that it's over is very hard. (Jeannie)

I just felt like I must not be doing enough for him to give to me. So I did more and more and more until there was just nothing left. (Becky)

TURNING TO SELF

How do women ever shift out of a preexisting, always already there, societal structure? Women get ingrained with so much gender programming to take care of other people, to put others first, to try to make others happy, that they do not turn back to themselves until they have no other choice, until they believe that continuing in the same direction will emotionally or physically kill them. They get to the point of thinking that "If I stay in this relationship I will fall apart physically or mentally." It is experienced as a survival issue; if they do not begin to take care of themselves, they will not make it. At that point, in spite of all the societal programming, they turn to their own resources as the only resources they have, the only way they think they might make it. As one of the therapists who reviewed the study said, "They just cannot do anything else besides change in some way. They get so far down that they must shift. In psychological abuse, they have to go even lower than in physical abuse."

Not until after I was hospitalized the second year in a row did I begin to realize that I could not save others anymore, that I had nothing left to give. I realized that my marriage had fallen apart years and years before, that the same issues [had] existed even when we dated. I knew that I never really had what I pretended to have, and that was someone that finally loved and cared for me. It hit me hard! (from Carol's written life story)

Every night when I would come in from work, he would just totally berate and downgrade me, criticize constantly. My son has said, "Mom, I've seen you get out of that car when you come in at night. I've seen you get out of that car in the driveway. You look perfectly happy and by the time you walk in that front door you look like your last friend has died."
    I told myself, I left for my own sanity. I didn't want a divorce. I don't even like the word divorce. I don't think that's the way things ought to be, but I actually had to leave for my own sanity. (Martha)

Often for the first time in their lives, instead of looking to a man to provide them with happiness, security, and love, the women started to look to themselves. In Jeannie's written life story, she titled this period "Coming Out":

I started thinking about me, my future, and what I wanted. I finally realized that no matter what I did, it wouldn't make him happy. A while ago I was in Overeaters Anonymous. The twelve steps helped me a lot, particularly in spiritual growth. I think it was the Serenity Prayer. I began to realize that the only person I could change was myself.

This major shift from focus on others to concern for self was reported by the other women.

Some of the things I'm trying to slowly do is establish my own world, my own life, instead of having it revolve around him. I don't want to live in a marriage where I'm not supported, where I'm not nurtured, where I am the caretaker all the time. I want some things given back and whether I can give it back to myself, you know, I have to have that. I know I'm not going to get it from him. (Betty)

What it finally came down to is that I was more important than him. I was more important than the relationship. I was more important than anything. (Tammi)

The only one I can help or change is me. A changed me is not what my family, my husband, or my children want. I have to cut loose of the ties that strangle me. It's the only hope of saving anyone! I can't go back, I can only go forward. (from Carol's written life story)

You have to be happy within yourself, and I knew I wasn't. I was miserable. And I just decided that I didn't want that relationship anymore. (Veronica)

By the time I asked him to move out, the tables had turned. I finally had the strength to say enough is enough. For my own sake as well as my kids, I knew I had to do something. (from Jeannie's written life story)

THE IMPORTANCE OF SUPPORT

With the shift to self for satisfaction, the women became less emotionally involved with their husbands; however, the decision to leave the relationship was still a frightening one. For all the participants, external support was necessary before they were able to leave; someone else had to identify the relationship as abusive and offer support and understanding. Outside support of her and condemnation of him was identified by Ferraro and Johnson (1983) as a catalyst for change in physically abusive relationships. This outside support is an even more essential catalyst in psychologically abusive relationships because the abuse does not leave visible scars and the husbands constantly tell them nothing is wrong.

Frequently the support came from their psychotherapist.

She [her psychotherapist] wanted me to go to a Women's Shelter for Abused Victims and, of course, I went off the deep end. That's when I think I realized that it was as serious as it was. That she wanted me to get my kids and take them to a shelter with me and stay away from him.

I decided that if I didn't stay away from him, that I was virtually going to be dead because I was already getting that way emotionally. I could not function. I don't think I could have told him to leave had I not been in counseling every day and had that support. (Carol)

Here's the turning point, the doctor said to me, "You don't really want to be treated like he treats you, do you? My last bit of advice to you is to go and get an attorney." (Dorothy)

I had been contemplating it for months, but was scared to death to do anything. It wasn't until talking to [her counselor], over and over and over that I decided that I did deserve better, and there's no reason to let him abuse me. But it took a long time to build up the confidence and self-esteem to finally get him out. (Rebecca)

For some of the women, the support they needed came from realizing that there were people who cared for them and who thought the relationship was abusive and who supported their decisions.

My sister saw what was going on and she said, "You gotta get out of here." ... I knew something had been wrong for a long time, but until she said it I thought, "Well, maybe it's just in my mind. Maybe I'm just imagining something is wrong, because he told me nothing is wrong." He told me that many times. He told me he didn't see anything wrong with verbally abusing people. As long as you don't hit them, you're fine. (Amy)

Then my friend started feeding me tapes and I'd play them in the car as I was driving. I used to get tickled because I'd come home from being on the road and he would say, "God, what's happened to you? You're an entirely different person." Well, I'd been listening to those tapes. On the tape Wayne Dyer said, "If you are married to someone because you think that's what you are supposed to be doing and there isn't trust and all of those elements involved, then I feel very sorry for you." I kept hearing that all the time. (Vicky)

My friend was a real strong, definite person in terms of what was right and what was wrong. She was really a good support for me. I would share and she would say, "Well, you don't have to stay here." It was like permission to get out. (Laura)

I think he [a man she dated after the separation] was put in my life at that point . . . for me to be able to break those bonds that I had with my ex-husband, that dependency, that real codependency on him. I mean, he's such a manipulator that I don't think I would have ever broken away. I think I would have just kept accepting more and more of the craziness of the whole situation and just gone on till he decided to end all relationships with me. (Debbi)

My mother treated me nice and loved me unconditionally. After a week of visiting, I was just dreading taking her to the airport and I was thinking about how I was living. How miserable I was, how I was tired of being treated the way I was being treated. When I said good-bye to her at the airport, I started crying and I couldn't stop. And I just kept thinking, "I want out, I want out." That was the turning point. (Laura)

I had met someone else [a man from work that she had become friends with]. I didn't know if it would work or not, but I said at least this gives me strength to do what I've been wanting to do and what I should have done a long time ago. That's when I moved out. (Angela)

Several women identified that just having the opportunity to tell their story and to be heard by me was supportive to them. According to Betty, "Going through this with you has helped me." Jeannie expressed relief in our third meeting; "I'm beyond all the intense feelings. That's happened since the last time I talked to you. I think it was useful to go over all that material with you."

Group support was critical to several of the participants. Within a group, women have an opportunity to realize that their experiences are similar to those of many other women. As one woman pointed out, "Their four walls are different, but the same thing was happening to them. Finally somebody was telling me what I've been through." Another woman learned from being in an all-women group. She saw the other women in the group as very knowledgeable, wise, and strong; her mother had had none of these qualities and neither had women she had associated with previously. The group was very important to her: "That's where my sanity lay. It depended on my being at those meetings. 'I would get better, things would change.' I knew that from the first meeting." Participation in group activity was empowering and led to changes in the women's thinking about themselves, their partners, and their relationships.

They [her psychotherapy group] give me healthy feedback that I don't get elsewhere. They make a good sounding board whether I'm being reasonable or unreasonable or whatever. (Rebecca)

After I began going to [a women's support group], I got the feeling from everyone else that I could hang up on him, I didn't have to sit there and take that anymore. I didn't have to buy into it or believe it anymore. It's real hard not to, it's like ingrained. It's like in granite up there, some of the things that he said to me. In the last year since I've been going to [the women's support group], I am much less anxious. (Dorothy)

LEAVING HOME

As these women gained more internal strength, they began to be able to set limits on how much they would take from their husbands. Often still hoping that maybe the relationship could be saved, many of the women identified a boundary beyond which they would end the relationship. They had moved from believing they could not survive without him to realizing they could not survive with him; but still they needed a final excuse to justify leaving, some final straw.

I began hating him soon after the marriage. I had decided that I would leave if the problems started to affect my daughter. That began last summer, but I wasn't strong enough mentally to leave him. (Amy)

I had given him the card for the clinic and I said that there were serious problems in our relationship and that I wanted to work on this marriage and that I hoped that he wanted to too, but if he didn't, that I knew that I had to leave to survive and that I would file for divorce. And I said, "I will give you two weeks from this date to find some kind of counseling, to talk to our minister, to talk to our friends, to find some kind of help somewhere." I said, "It doesn't have to be my counselor, but we have to be in counseling, 'cause it's not going to work unless we do. If you do not, I am going to file for divorce." He threw the card in the trash. He wasn't going to do it. I cried a lot. I did not talk to him anymore about it. I did not mention it to him anymore. After the two week period was over, I had already contacted attorneys and I had hired one. (Carol)

I told him that if he stayed out all night, that he might as well just not bother to come back. . . . Then he was gone all night one night. The next day I went to see a lawyer and three weeks later he was gone. (Jeannie)

If it had just been he and I, I probably would have suffered a lot longer, but when it came to him hurting [their daughter], I couldn't tolerate that. . . . He was just so abusive emotionally to her, you know, and once physically. It's like, she doesn't need that and she's young enough that I hope she doesn't remember. I mean, this is what I'm thinking at the time, that it would be better for her now and she may not remember it then. I just couldn't see putting her through everything. If I'd had my way, now, looking back, I would have left as soon as he threw her [he threw her on their bed]. You know, I wouldn't have let it go on. He would have been gone that instant if I hadn't been so scared. (Rebecca)

Before actually ending the relationship, the women had made many major changes. They had accepted their desperate position, turned to themselves for strength, gained support from someone else, and identified a final condition. They had also created or believed they could create an alternative way of living, could take care of themselves. They created new narratives for their lives, ones that were not dependent on a relationship with a man. Interestingly, the younger women were able to move out of psychologically abusive relationships sooner than the older women; it was easier for them to create powerful and believable alternative stories since, even if they came from a very traditional background, they knew women who were making it independently.

For all these women, the process of actually leaving the relationship was like leaving home, but more frightening because they were leaving everything that home stands for and moving to a totally different way of understanding life. They had given up on the fantasy that they would be taken care of by a man and that the woman could and should make everything okay. The women experienced leaving as a wrenching process.

It's just that I've been there with him so long. I feel so uneasy about everything because I left house, job, relatives, family, friends, and town. (Becky)

I worked with my husband for eighteen years in a family business. I mean I had anxiety so badly until recently that it was very difficult to be social at all. (Dorothy)

I'm realizing that I had no identity as a child either so I didn't know what it was like. I just went into a marriage and that was just natural for me and now I am beginning to discover myself. It is a very scary thing. It is scary to take steps out on your own and to try to figure out what you want and who you are, because you were always somebody or something that somebody always wanted you to be. (Carol)

The process of leaving home often did not stop when the relationship ended with the husband. As if society just cannot stand the idea of women functioning adequately alone, in many cases their families of origin began trying to dominate their lives, and their ex-husbands still parented them.

My dad controlled me when I was growing up, he is still trying to do it. My husband tried controlling me and I'm done with that. He still keeps trying to do that. He says, "You are going to need a car soon, you should look at the Saturns because that is what you can afford." (Angela)

I'm having the very same problem with my father and he was the one that controlled everything when we were kids. After my divorce, I started making some of my own decisions and doing things on my own and he would get upset. Then he would get my mom upset because I would leave the house and they wouldn't know where I was. You know, I was supposed to tell somebody where I was and exactly which direction I went. (Carol)

Most of the women in this study had left the abusive relationship by the time I talked to them. But sometimes leaving did not stop the abuse.

He was very verbally abusive to me when he found out I was dating. I mean he stood on my driveway and he just absolutely ran me up and down and round about. My neighbors were sitting on the opposite side of the fence from him. She called me after he left and I don't even know these people very much. She said, "It was all I could do to keep my husband from opening that gate up and tearing into him." She said, "I cannot believe the things he said to you." (Debbi)

In most cases, the husbands continued the abusive behavior during the divorce. They seemed to have trouble accepting that their wives would actually get a divorce.

One time when he came over, he started yelling at me and telling me that I needed to stop all this nonsense and that I needed to give up on some of these things that I was fighting for. I wouldn't talk to him. I said, "Get out of my house." He says, "It's not your house, yet." I said, "You leave this house or I'll call the police." And he goes, "Well, what are we going to do about settling this?" I said, "Your attorney can talk to my attorney. Get out of my house." And he did leave and after that, he never did bother me again about anything. (Carol)

In many cases, one of the children—most frequently the oldest son—followed the father's example of abuse. This pattern of the son assuming the role of his abusing father has also been seen in physically abusive relationships (Pizzey 1974).

He started just breaking curfew, breaking all the rules, giving me a hard time. I'd take his car keys away and then one day he wrestled me to the ground to get his car keys. I said, "You walk out of this door and I'm calling the police." He said, "That's just great. You called the police on your husband, then you call the police on your son." I said, "Yeah, I will."

When he walked out the door, it was over, so I called and I had him picked up 'cause I said the car was not in his name. He was furious about that. He said he wasn't going to put up with it. I said, "Well, neither am I." He left in the car again. While he was gone, I packed all of his stuff. I had everything off the wall, packed everything. I cried the whole time. What ended up happening is that [son] started treating me the exact same way that his dad did. That's what was so scary. . . . It just amazes me how he sounds like his dad. (Carol)

Our son, who was three years old at the time, he began talking to me the way he saw his father talking to me. That was one of the things that turned the light on in my head, he's learning his father's behavior. He's learning how to be a huntsman and I decided, you know, I can't have him treating me like his father treats me. (Laura)

I have a little nine-year-old daughter. She's almost ten, but I noticed any time he was around, she would slip over to his way of behavior toward me. (Becky)

A pattern frequently found in physically abusive relationships but not common in psychologically abusive relationships is returning to the relationship many times before leaving for good. The women leave because they have been physically hurt, but they may not have hit bottom and given up emotionally. In psychologically abusive relationships, the women do not leave until they have given up emotionally, turned to themselves for satisfaction, and gained external support. When they do leave, there is no shift in their husbands. He does not beg her to return or vow to change. He continues to maintain that it is all her fault, proving to her once again that he is not going to change. For many of the women in this study, it took a long time to decide to leave, but once the decision was made, the relationship was over.

I thought about it long enough before leaving. It was like I knew it was just over by then. Plus when I left, you would expect someone to say, don't leave me or please, I love you, come back. He never said a word to me. (Angela)

When I told him I was going to leave, . . . he spent two hours telling me what all I had to do to change in order to stay. I didn't ask him to stay, I told him I was going to leave. And yet he spent two hours telling me how I had to change in order to stay. (Martha)

STARTING OVER

Even with the continued abuse and often serious financial problems, starting over was a liberating experience. The strength these women had gained was valuable in handling the ongoing problems.

It's an eerie feeling. I hate even thinking about it 'cause that's the hardest part I had with him was breaking away from that hold. Eventually when we would talk after I left him, I got to the point where I was able to say, "I want you to know, I will not let you manipulate me. You're not going to persuade me in any way." It probably did nothing for him for me to say that, but, for me, hearing myself say that helped a lot. (Amy)

I was finally a person and he was not taking it away from me again. I really don't think my husband believed I could stick it out and make it on my own. About two to four weeks after I asked him to move out, he filed for divorce. It was a scare tactic that didn't work. (from Jeannie's written life story)

I was angry at first, very angry for him not calling [their son]. It was hurting me. I would sit and cry, but then I said," I can't do this 'cause I can't change him." I left him because I couldn't change him and I couldn't control what he was doing. I couldn't live with it, so I left. And now I can't expect to change that again. (Angela)

I felt pretty confident at the end that I was making the right decision and that I don't need to live in this abusive household, nor do I need to let [their daughter] be at risk to that. I felt much stronger in that sense, in what I didn't want with him, but I was scared of what the future held because I was two months pregnant and I knew [their daughter] was going to have her [serious type of] surgery. You know, with money and insurance and stuff and the house, I was real fearful of what would occur in the future. But, in that moment in time, I felt like I owned the world 'cause I made the decision and I kicked him out and that was really hard for me to do. (Rebecca)

With some break from the abuse, the women began to heal more quickly, to feel positive about their lives, to be glad that they were starting over.

I've been with him for twenty years. You know, it's sort of like waking up and starting over again. Maybe today will be different. (Kathy)

Before I was consumed by it, I was critical if I didn't do everything just right. Now I'm using the Serenity Prayer and some of the material from the twelve steps. I think for it to work, you first must accept where you are. Before, I was still trying to change him or me. It is like all of a sudden all the pain lifted. I don't know for sure what happened. I guess it was the praying and the Serenity Prayer and knowing I could make it.

I feel ready to start over, to make new friends, to get on with my life. It's been two and a half years since we were separated. I feel I've reached a plateau. (Jeannie)

The reason I got out is because hopefully I'm liking myself more and I've got my kids to consider and realize that I don't have to have a man in my life, especially an abusive one. (Rebecca)

Most physically battered women are optimistic about the possibility of satisfying future relationships with men (Scanzoni 1972). This sense of hope is not as common among psychologically abused women, who tend to be very hesitant about trusting another man. Although several of the women have now been divorced for a while, only one of the sixteen has remarried.

I guess I could be sexually involved, but I don't want to be emotionally involved. I don't want to be hurt again. I want to protect myself from emotional involvement, but I know I can't hide from that forever. The men [that she has dated] sure did make me feel good about me. I liked the compliments. (Jeannie)

This is the first time that I haven't been interested in or wanting another companion. And that, for a lot of reasons, feels really good. There is still so much that I want to learn and, you know, I have to treat myself to before I want to share myself with anybody else. And I've just got too many things going on right now that I don't have mental energy to put into a relationship. That's a real revelation in me, not feeling that I have to have somebody to take care of me. (Rebecca)

If I ever do remarry, I will know the red flags to look for because I don't want another relationship like I had. I do not want to be walked on and I'm now starting to stick up for myself. You know, if someone says something to me that I don't like, I say, "Hey, I don't like that." I can stop it like that. (Veronica)

Several of the women in the study had gotten to the point of seeing themselves as finally free from the abusive relationship. Their stories had changed completely from the "happily ever after" tales they had imagined when they got married. Jeannie titled the current chapter of her written life history, "I win, I'm free." The others who had left the relationships and gotten to a point of emotional freedom expressed similar thoughts.

Recovery is my priority. I finally became more important than him. He will be the last one, the last abuser. Any kind of abuse is totally unacceptable to me now. I'm finally getting a life, a decent life, a sane life .... Priorities now are my health, mentally, emotionally, spiritually. I love to exercise, read, work, have time to myself. I love to see my daughter and grandchildren and spend time with them. I love to see my friends. I love sanity and I will continue recovery for the rest of my life. I love to write in my journal and I love to learn. I love music, my cat, my [specific type of car]. Above all I love me. Finally. P.S. I love to dance. (from Tammi's written life story)

Although looking back helps me go forward, going back would kill me. I know I cannot go back to a way of life that was choking the life out of me. Going forward is extremely painful, but the pain is that which brings healing, hope, and happiness. I have experienced that feeling of "being" and I can never go back. There was nothing of me there. I can only experience me by moving through pain and hurt, but on the other side waits joy and hope! On the other side waits me! (from Carol's written life story)

When you live in such craziness so long, upheaval and turmoil is normal and when there is some serenity, it almost gets boring. (Debbi)

I feel better. It is like a weight off my shoulders doing what I want to do, when I want to do it, doing fun things, taking my son places, not resenting my husband for not being there with us. (Angela)

I think it is much more peaceful, a lot more peaceful, a lot more serenity .... I do a lot more things than I ever did when we were married. I've been to the ballet, I've been to lots of movies which I love to do. I go out to eat a lot. I do a lot more things. (Veronica)

I learned a great deal from each of these women. It was exciting to trace their evolutions as they moved from self-blame and sole responsibility for the relationship problems to an awareness that their view of reality had value and that they could take care of themselves. For some, the process was completed more quickly, but for most it took many years to face the risks, to walk through the myriad of transitions that led to blossoming. It was a difficult and painful journey for each woman.

10

TREATMENT RECOMMENDATIONS

I wanted to go to a therapist, but he wouldn't let me. He said he was my therapist. He wouldn't give me money to go to a therapist. (24-year-old unemployed woman whose husband had a middle-class income)

He wanted me to call somebody but not a counselor. He'd say, "I don't need a counselor. They just take your money. It's a waste of my time." So I went for several months to her anyway because I just had to do it to get out of bed. He was very critical of it. (37-year-old mother of two children)

Psychologically abused women, like physically abused women, present difficult challenges for clinicians. In her work with physically abused women Burstow (1992) states, "frustration comes from caring, overinvolvement, and oversimplification" (153). The same can be said of working with psychologically abused women. The clinician must remember that an abused woman has been told daily for years that she is inadequate, that the problems are all her fault, that she deserves the treatment she gets, that she is lucky that he does not beat her. She needs patience and reassurance that nothing she has done justifies being abused. She needs a therapist who will counter the abuse by affirming her reality, taking the abuse seriously, and accepting the damage done by psychological abuse.

The journey, which begins by naming the problems in the relationships and gradually moves to owning her power to create a satisfying life, is often slow and always frightening. Therapists who understand the typical process in psychologically abusive relationships have a distinct advantage in helping a woman move through this evolution. They realize that a woman in the early stages of the relationship might present herself as to blame for all the problems in the relationship. Later she might present herself as a victim of his abusive behavior, as a person who needs help in moving to a position of assertiveness and responsibility for creating a satisfying life. For every psychologically abused woman, the long-term goal needs to be to become a strong, active agent in the creation of her own life.

DIFFERENCES BETWEEN PHYSICALLY AND PSYCHOLOGICALLY ABUSIVE RELATIONSHIPS

When working with psychologically abused women, it is important to keep in mind the differences between physically abusive relationships, which are usually also psychologically abusive, and psychologically abusive relationships. A critical and obvious difference is that there is no visible evidence of damage in psychologically abusive relationships. This means that it is easier for both partners to deny the damage and that it takes much longer for others to recognize the damage (Ferraro 1979). With psychological abuse, he may appear innocent not only to himself but also to others. His guilt is much harder to hide if he has physically hurt her.

Since in physically abusive relationships, she may require protective shelter or medical intervention because of physical injury (Ferraro 1979; Koslof 1984), the shift from private troubles to public involvement comes earlier than with psychological abuse. It is often years, however, before either the wife or the professionals recognize that her depression, anxiety, and/or psychosomatic illness is related to ongoing psychological abuse. Although our society accepts men dominating women and children, there is less acceptance for physical injury (Ferraro 1979). Having incorporated the societal standards, men who physically abuse women may blame her for provoking him (Anderson and

Rouse 1988); but they eventually express guilt and remorse, promising to change (Ferraro 1979; Walker 1979). These attempts to change create honeymoon periods when he is trying to win her back (Ferraro and Johnson 1983; Pfouts 1978; Walker 1979). During these periods, she is hopeful that the relationship can be saved. Our society tends to be accepting, unwilling to see, or much less critical of psychological abuse, so men who psychologically abuse women believe that their behavior is justified. In fact, men who are psychologically abusive define their behavior as appropriate and make no attempt to change; therefore, psychological abuse is ongoing. Physical abuse is episodic (Moore 1979; Walker 1979); psychological abuse is continuous.

There are also differences at the end of the relationship. Women who are physically abused typically leave the relationship many times. Early separations occur at times of physical injury, fear, and/or anger. Since emotional attachment is still strong (Burstow 1992; Henson and Schinderman 1981), there are many attempts to reconcile (Burstow 1992; Ferraro 1983; Gelles 1976; Pagelow 1981; Symonds 1979). Women in psychologically abusive relationships do not leave until they hit bottom emotionally, have little attachment left, and have begun to develop new internal and external supports. They do not attempt to reconcile. The emotional damage in psychologically abusive relationships is so severe that the women are very hesitant to make a commitment to another relationship. On the other hand, women who have been physically abused are optimistic about the possibility of future satisfying relationships with men (Scanzoni 1972).

Abusive Relationships: Summary of Differences

Psychological Abuse	Physical Abuse
No visible evidence of abuse	Visible evidence of abuse
Abuse hidden from others	Abuse evident to others
He appears innocent	He appears guilty
Shift from private to public avoided	Shift from private to public necessary because of injury or need for protection

Society accepts abuse	Society condemns abuse
He believes his behavior is justified	He expresses guilt and remorse
Others ignore his behavior	Others are critical of his behavior
He does not attempt to change	He attempts to change
Abuse is continuous	Abuse is episodic
She detaches emotionally before separating	She first separates while emotionally attached
No attempts to reconcile after she ends relationship	Many attempts to reconcile
She is hesitant to commit to another relationship	She is optimistic about future relationships

---

TREATMENT PROCESS

With an understanding of psychological abuse, clinicians can listen and watch for indications of psychological abuse beginning with the assessment interview. Assessment of married women who are depressed, anxious, and/or have psychosomatic symptoms should include the possibility of psychological abuse. If psychological abuse seems possible, patterns of domination, economic deprivation or excessive control, social isolation, verbal attacking and criticism, and/or withdrawal and lack of emotional connection can be explored.

Early in therapy, the client needs to describe the relationship and gradually realize that it is psychologically abusive. Initially, women often trivialize or understate the problems. They may be protecting their partners' images or believing that the problems are really all their fault. This trivialization of the relationship problems can be seen as part of being socialized as feminine, of having been taught that they are less important and should accept and make do (Burstow 1992). The women are convinced that they are lucky that their husbands stay with them. Over the years they normalize their problems and depression.

During this beginning phase of the work, it is important that the therapist identify the abuse and express appropriate shock and concern about the painful aspects of the relationship. It is also helpful and often empowering to name the woman's experience as psychological abuse (Pozatek 1994; Tolman 1992). This naming and empathic understanding helps the woman to maintain her often shaky belief that something is seriously wrong with the relationship. She needs feedback, validation, empathy, understanding, and acceptance of her decisions. Validating her reality is essential and must often be done many times as she gradually gains or regains confidence in her own view of the situation.

Waiting while the client moves through the process at her own pace can be frustrating. The therapist can easily become a subtle abuser, pushing the client to accept the therapist's view of reality and subtly criticizing the client for not changing. This action on the part of the therapist is experienced by the client as lack of understanding. What psychologically abused women need is to know they can talk about their pain without therapists pressuring them to take any action before they are ready.

Instead of pushing for change, the therapist needs to counteract the lack of validation in the relationship by inviting the client to focus on her reality. What does she think? What does she want? How does she feel? As the therapist listens to the client and supports her perceptions, the client will begin the process of reclaiming self. As she shares her story, new meanings can be constructed that highlight her strengths, her beliefs and values, and that look toward the creation of future satisfaction.

As the client searches for new meanings and understandings, she will need to face the entrapping interaction patterns that exist between herself and her partner and gradually figure out how to escape from what has been identified as an inescapable situation. She will have to develop a plan of action other than doing nothing, overadaptation, agitation, violence, or incapacitation, since these behaviors are all passive and leave the other person in charge (Schiff 1975). It may take a long time for her to get to the point of accepting that no matter what she does her partner will not be satisfied with her, will not give her the recognition she craves. She will have to turn to external supporters and to herself, eventually owning her worth, importance, and validity no matter what he says or does.

Some of the women in this study moved from blaming themselves for the problems in the relationship to blaming something else. This was particularly common when the abuser was an alcoholic or came from an abusive background; the abuser was then absolved from personal responsibility and the disease or his background was blamed. The women felt they had to be understanding and nurturing to their husbands, who were now put in the position of distressed victims of their disease or of their oppressive childhood. This understanding stance may get expressed in the belief that his alcoholism and/or childhood abuse is responsible for and justifies his abuse of her. The therapist needs to continually focus back to the woman herself. She cannot do anything to solve his problem; she must focus on solving her own entrapment. She must realize that her husband has responsibility for dealing appropriately with the people in his life now.

A central question in this work is: What triggers the shift from self-blame to identifying the relationship as abusive and beginning the long process to freedom? In every case the constellation of variables will be unique, but some groups of the following factors will be present: an increase in abusiveness or behavior beyond some preestablished limit, a refocusing on her own potential, an identification of the relationship as abusive by some significant external person, and/or the possibility of an improved situation away from the marriage. In most cases, the turning point does not come until the woman becomes desperate, until she comes to a place of believing that she cannot continue in the relationship—not that she has the choice to continue or does not want to continue, but that she cannot continue, that staying is destroying her health and sanity. At that point, she stops looking to her husband to provide her with whatever she needs and begins to rely on herself, to claim her own agency and power.

In order to achieve this internal stability, most women need to look at the problem from the broad point of view of society, to comprehend how she was invited into an imbalanced relationship and a position of powerlessness by our patriarchal society.

This perspective leads to understanding the power of gender, to rejecting the limitations imposed by gender, and to accepting her uniqueness as an individual.

Psychotherapists have been accused of locating the deficiencies in the individual rather than in our capitalist patriarchal system (Langman 1991). We need to increase our critique of capitalist patriarchy, which is particularly destructive to women and children. A commitment to changing the level of psychological abuse of women in marriage must also involve advocating for changes at a societal level. As long as our society supports women living through their children and discourages men from taking an active role in parenting, "women will continue to bring up sons whose sexual identity depends on devaluing femininity inside and outside themselves" (Chodorow 1989, 44). We need to move to a family structure characterized by role symmetry, with both sexes engaged in instrumental and expressive tasks and in working and nurturing (Boss and Thorne 1991; Walters et al. 1988) and to a societal system that creates a balance of all types of power. At a societal level, ending psychological abuse of women can only be done if we eliminate the prevailing patriarchal patterns of gender which establish men as dominant and women as submissive.

THERAPY WITH COUPLES

Psychotherapists working with couples should be alert to the possibility of hidden psychological abuse. Both husband and wife may believe that it is her responsibility to keep him happy and make the relationship work. When working with a couple, the therapist may choose to challenge this thinking by inviting both partners to identify what they are doing to promote happiness and closeness in the relationship. This line of inquiry acts as an important message about joint responsibility for the health of the relationship.

Some of the psychotherapists the women in this study had encountered noticed the husbands' covert agendas and reached for a contract for change from them. A few of the psychotherapists seemed to have missed the husband's involvement in the problem and accepted the husband's identification that the relationship problems were the wife's fault and that he was only along to help the therapist "fix" her. The participants reported that their husbands maintained a "strong, silent, there is nothing wrong with me" stance to the therapist. One of the psychotherapists who reviewed this study said,

I think the biggest tip-off is when somebody comes in and is willing to be very helpful and doesn't have much self-interest. If they come in with too little self-interest, then they have already given you their hand.

Commenting on the husband's stance will help to validate the wife's reality. The therapist needs to accept the separate constructions of reality of the husband and the wife, to encourage each person to identify the strengths in the partner, and to help the couple reach an agreement on the kind of marriage they want. This agreement can be the goal of their work together. After these elements have been accomplished, a narrative approach (White & Epston 1990) which allows the therapist to separate the problem from the individuals is more likely to be accepted than a more confrontational approach.

Being knowledgeable about the interaction patterns that exist in psychologically abusive relationships is important for any therapist who is working with couples. As a part of the assessment, the therapist should look for indications of complementary schismogenesis. Does she become submissive in reaction to a minimal stimulus such as a glance on his part? Indications of a double bind involve a belief on her part that she cannot comment on the conflicting messages. This is most evident with regard to messages about closeness: does he attack her for withdrawing in any way and also attack her if she initiates closeness?

Finding out about the existence of direct verbal attacks can be difficult with both partners present, since anything the wife reports that is negative is often used by the husband to attack her later. Use of checklists such as the Conflict Tactics Scale (Straus 1979), the Index of Spouse Abuse (Hudson and McIntosh 1981), or the Psychological Maltreatment of Women Inventory (Tolman 1989) can be helpful to the therapist and the client in gaining a clearer assessment of the level of abuse. However, if the therapist believes the relationship may be abusive, she should do at least some of the assessment in individual appointments. An assessment of the use of silence as a punishment and control tactic is also more safely done in individual appointments.

INTRAPERSONAL TREATMENT

After facing the role of society in the creation of their powerless position, many women will choose to explore the internal dynamics of the problem. This should be postponed until the woman has gained enough strength and personal agency that she will not use such a focus to revert to self-blaming. When working with an abused woman at an intrapsychic level, the therapist might choose to relate current abuse to childhood problems and facilitate resolution of these earlier issues related to abuse. Many of the women in this study reported that their parents' marriages were psychologically abusive, and in two cases there was also physical abuse. Most of the women felt ignored by their parents, some identified that they were psychologically abused by their parents, and physical abuse was present in two cases. None of the women had mothers who modeled anything other than dysfunctional patterns or traditional gender behavior.

If a woman chooses to understand intrapsychic dynamics related to her abusive relationship, the therapist could use the work of the French psychoanalyst Lacan (1977), who examined how unconscious images structure perception of current relationships. Women who grew up with images of the all-powerful fathers learn that men are in the position of authority, the "subject presumed to know." Lacan's discourse on interpretation and transference is uniquely helpful in understanding the position of women. Interpretation, which "is always the exercise of power" (Gallop 1985, 27), is present every time one person explains or defines reality to another person. The person with authority—the man, the husband, the therapist—is viewed "as 'a subject presumed to know'—as the very place where meaning resides" (Felman 1977, 7). He defines truth and establishes meaning, including what is true and meaningful about her. In abusive relationships, the husband defines her reality and refutes her sense of truth any time it does not agree with his. Even her internal experiences are often challenged, leaving her feeling unsure and confused.

Lacan identifies that whenever the structure of a relationship includes a "subject presumed to know," transference will be the effect (Gallop 1985). Traditional "man and wife" relationships are structured, at least partly, by transference. Just as with the therapist, the wife projects power onto her husband. He acts out this power, enhancing his prestige and minimizing her. As women gain an understanding of this mechanism, they can understand and change their role in the power imbalance that exists in psychologically abusive marriages.

Another powerful Lacanian concept is the imaginary, which is made up of imagoes: unconscious images that structure the way a person perceives others. Perception of the other is constructed by projection of specific imagoes. Women may project the imago of the Father onto their husband, seeing him as the omniscient definer of reality. He is identified as having the stronger ego and she identifies with him, accepting his image of reality in place of her own. After recognizing the effect of the client's imagoes on current relationships, one of the goals of Lacanian psychoanalysis is for the client to realize that the projected imagoes are part of the imaginary.

Lacan attacks ego psychology as becoming mired in the imaginary. By inviting the client to identify with the "stronger" ego of the therapist, the client misses the chance to gain understanding of her imagoes. She simply takes on the therapist imago, which is certified by the therapist as reality (Gallop 1985). Ego psychology authorizes the therapist to "act out the transferential illusion, becoming the good, strong parent, the ultimate role model" (Gallop 1985, 29). These therapists do not question the imaginary structuring of this relationship or look at "how it minoritized the patient and enhanced the analyst's self-deluded prestige" (Gallop 1985, 29). This relationship played out over and over between authoritarian or powerful therapists and female clients repeats the oppression and denigration of women.

Lacan theorizes that only when the analyst is truly neutral can she be a mirror for the client. The client can then see and take ownership of her projections, realizing that the mirror has no content. To move from the imaginary to the symbolic, the client must understand the imaginary as imaginary, be able to "look into the mirror and see not the image but the mirror itself" (Gallop 1985, 62). Being able to look at a man and see the man—instead of authority, truth, power, reality, knowledge, or the source of happiness—is the essence of psychological liberation for women.

If clients are invited or allowed to see the therapist as the powerful one, they will once again perceive the power as outside of self and accept someone else's definition of reality. This power imbalance is oppressive. Instead the client should experience self-definition, self-confirmation, and self-direction within the therapy process (Bepko 1989). The client can be helped to see that the power is not in the therapist, the interpretation, or the husband but endowed by her.

The clinician must validate and support the client's definition of her reality and must consistently invite her to reclaim her projections, to own her power. Whatever model or form of therapy is used, one of the goals must be for the woman to be able to perceive herself as the source of her truth, her happiness, her reality, her power, her authority, her sense of well-being rather than seeing the source as external.

In order to establish a sense of personal power, women must reown their anger. Women have learned that aggression and anger are unfeminine and therefore unacceptable. They often suppress their anger and become depressed (Ball and Wyman 1978) or repress anger and become anxious. They need a supportive environment in which the expression and understanding of anger is allowed and encouraged, one in which manifestations of anger are understood as necessary when moving away from toxic situations and when needing to maintain powerful positions.

As therapists, we must help abused women envision and create a reality that is not abusive. In some cases, this means leaving an abusive husband, sometimes even moving to another location. As one of the therapists who read the summary said, "It is like leaving home in all senses of that word and moving to another country where you don't know the language, you look different, and you wear different clothes." It is leaving psychologically all that was home in terms of how life is supposed to be. Leaving abuse is a hard, long journey; but it is worth the effort.

Maybe leaving home is a foundation step to a grander goal.

Another French psychoanalyst, Luce Irigaray (1985b), sees the goal as constructing a singular, separate, unique, different, and powerful position for women. Irigaray (1985b) posits "pure difference," not difference from one positive term, or women as different from men; but altogether different as *A* is different from *B* rather than *A* is different from *A-* or not-*A*. Irigaray's project is the development of accounts of subjectivity and knowledge that acknowledge the existence of two different sexes, two different bodies, two different forms of desire and ways of knowing, and two different languages (Grosz 1990). In *Speculum of the Other Women* (Irigaray 1985a), she says, "If only your ears were not so formless, so clogged with meaning(s), that they are closed to what does not in some way echo the already heard" (113). Maybe our ears have been closed to new possibilities, but we can find a way to open them so that we can help women who have been trapped in one-down, powerless, abused positions to envision a different reality, one with a new, strong, and healthy position for all women.

USEFUL THERAPEUTIC APPROACHES

Given the complex needs of women who have been psychologically abused, multiple forms of therapy are probably the most effective. The participants in this study used individual therapy, group therapy, and support groups. Whatever the form of therapy, an integral part of the process is the telling of her story. Her story will include her construction of herself and an account of her attempts to make sense of the paths she has chosen and followed, the successes and failures she has had, the joys and pains she has lived through (Gergen and Gergen 1983; Laird 1991b; McAdams 1993).

The value of the woman's story needs to be owned by the therapist and the client. Stories of survival, change, and accomplishment are critical to healing (Saleeby 1994). As these women heard other women's stories, they began to regain faith in their own perceptions and to believe that they too could create a more satisfying future. The women reported that as they heard similar stories, they learned about themselves and gained insight into the meaning of their lives. In the telling of her story, a woman can strengthen her understanding of what happened, identify her capacities, solidify her determination to create a different future, and offer other women a new story that they may use to transform their life. For therapists from the constructivist school, the generation of new stories that incorporate alternative knowledges and build on client strengths, abilities, and resources is considered central to the therapy process (Gallant 1993; White and Epston 1990).

Group therapy and/or support groups—particularly all-women groups (Aries 1976; Carlock and Martin 1977; Schubert-Walker 1981)—are particularly helpful to women who have been psychologically abused. In groups, women can tell their stories and have them validated as truth by other women who have had similar experiences. In the final meetings, several of the women commented on how helpful it was for them to read about others whose stories were the same. As Becky said, "I didn't say that but I could have. It was true of me." Dorothy commented, "There is something empowering about knowing it isn't just you."

Their involvement with the group also breaks the pattern of isolation. With the support of the group, women report being able to begin focusing some of their energy on self-nurturance. Gradually they begin to understand that meeting his standards for "wife" is impossible and destructive for them. Using information from others in the group, they can set new achievable and meaningful standards and stop being so self-critical. With this shift, his criticism seems less powerful and hurtful and his hold on her reality is broken.

Feminist therapy is useful in helping women address the societal aspects of the problem. "Feminist therapy is based on the belief that gender inequality is the underlying problem for women and that economic and psychological autonomy are essential factors for women's mental health and psychological well-being" (Kravetz 1986, 114). Feminist therapists use numerous therapeutic strategies to facilitate client empowerment, including assertiveness training, improving communication abilities, time management, and conflict resolution skills (Van Den Bergh and Cooper 1986). They attempt to minimize dependency, working to equalize the power between therapist and client. Clients are invited to understand therapeutic techniques and encouraged to critique approaches, values, and ideas of the therapists. Feminist therapists demonstrate their faith that women can and should be autonomous agents, in control of their lives (Kravetz 1986; Van Den Bergh and Cooper 1986). Clients of feminist therapists have reported the following helpful factors: seeing their therapist as a competent woman, knowing that their therapist has shared the female experience, and discovering that other women can be important and helpful in one's life (Johnson 1976).

Believing that women must understand the ways in which society has limited their autonomy and choice and participated in their oppression, feminist therapists include gender-role analysis, which is "a process through which women come to understand how, by internalizing cultural values about women, they become co-conspirators in their own oppression" (Kravetz 1986, 116). This understanding can be the foundation for constructing a self-image that is not limited by gender.

In psychologically abusive relationships, women lose whatever sense of personal power and agency they once had. In regaining a sense of power, they can benefit greatly from empowering activities. Since empowerment comes from active participation (Kieffer 1984; Rappaport 1981; Zimmerman 1990; Zimmerman and Rappaport 1988), being a part of a social action group or a consciousness-raising group can be very helpful to psychologically abused women. Studies of consciousness-raising groups show increases in sense of connection, relationship, and solidarity with other women; self-esteem, self-awareness, and self-respect; understanding of sexism, oppression, and gender roles; and participation in activities to improve the condition of women (Kravetz 1986). Within consciousness-raising groups, social relations can be demystified as individuals share experiences (Dominelli and McLeod 1989).

CLOSING THOUGHTS

In the final group meetings with the participants, I asked the women what advice they had for young women or women in psychologically abusive relationships. Their thoughts summarize what they learned on their journeys.

"Don't wait, it won't get any better," Angela mandated. She did not stay in the relationship for very long after deciding she could never get what she wanted in it.

Betty's advice was, "Be sure you can financially take care of yourself, that you are your own individual financially and emotionally before you get married." Betty has decided to stay in the relationship at least partly because her husband is a doctor and supports her quite well. She has not developed a career.

"Find your own identity, what you want to do, what makes you happy before you get married," offered Carol, who has left a very abusive relationship and is still struggling to maintain her independence against the constant pulls from her ex-husband and her family of origin, who live near her and criticize her for making decisions on her own. Dorothy, who got married right out of high school, had similar advice: "I certainly would want my children to live independently before marriage just to have that experience."

Laura wanted to remind other women that "you not only marry him but his family. Look at his relationship with his mother and his parents' marriage." Laura's ex-husband came from an abusive family.

Debbi is a college graduate who was beginning her career when she got married. She quit because her husband did not want her to work and because she could not work and give him the amount of attention he expected. She said, "They need to be financially able to care for themselves and maintain that through the marriage." Debbi is having to start over after many years of being out of the job market. She may never be able to establish the kind of career she is capable of having.

Tammi wanted to exhort women to unite.

You can't start blaming the other women because that's where society wants us. They want to pit us against each other. That's what they want us to do so that we won't unite. Because God forbid if we unite, we might have some power. For God sakes, we can't let women do that. We've got to pit them against each other so they call each other tramps and whores and sluts and whatever all so they [men] can have all the power still. They're still in control and they didn't do anything wrong. It's those crazy women over there that are fighting. It's nothing wrong with us, it's them.

Kathy told the group in the final meeting that her daughters had been blaming the woman their father was dating. Kathy set them straight:

Girls, your father is the one who left. I don't know if [the woman he was having an affair with] went after him; I don't know anything about [other women]. Your father is the one that made the decision to go. If he wanted to spurn her advances, if he was happy here, if this meant enough to him to tell her that this wasn't going to happen to him, he'd be here right now. I'm not going to blame her.

After years of hoping he would take care of her, Valerie counseled other women that "no one else can take care of you like you can." A final piece of wisdom came from Debbi, who summarized everything by saying, "Don't ever give the responsibility for your happiness to another person." As each of us follows that advice in our own life and works to create environments in which others can experience having responsibility for their own happiness, our world will change.

REFERENCES

Andersen, S. M. (1985). Identifying coercion and deception in social systems. In B. Kilbourner, ed., *Divergent perspectives on the new religions* (pp. 12–23). Washington, DC: American Association for the Advancement of Science.

Andersen, S. M., Boulette, T. R., and Schwartz, A. H. (1991). Psychological maltreatment of spouses. In R. T. Ammerman and M. Hersen, eds., *Case studies in family violence* (pp. 293–328). New York: Plenum.

Anderson, C., and Rouse, L. (1988). Intervention in cases of woman battering: An application of symbolic interactionism and critical theory. *Clinical Sociology Review* 6: 134–47.

Aries, E. (1976). Interaction patterns and themes of male, female and mixed groups. *Small Group Behavior* 7: 7–18.

Ball, P. G., and Wyman, E. (1978). Battered wives and powerlessness: What can counselors do? *Victimology* 2 (3–4): 545–52.

Balsamo, A. (1987). Un-wrapping the postmodern: A feminist glance. *Journal of Communication Inquiry* 11 (1): 64–72.

Barrett, M. (1988). *Women's oppression today: The Marxist/feminist encounter.* London: Verso.

Bartky, S. L. (1990). *Femininity and domination: Studies in the phenomenology of oppression.* New York: Routledge.

Basic, M. M. (1992). Reading the alcoholic film: Analysis of the *The Country Girl. The Sociological Quarterly* 33 (2): 211–27.

Bateson, G. P. (1972). *Steps to an ecology of the mind: Collected essays in anthropology, psychiatry, evolution, and epistemology.* San Francisco: Chandler.

Bell, C., and Newby, H. (1976). Husbands and wives: The dynamics of the deferential dialectic. In D. L. Barker and S. Allen, eds., *Dependence and exploitation in work and marriage* (pp. 152–68). New York: Longman.

Benjamin, J. (1988). *The bonds of love: Psychoanalysis, feminism, and the problem of domination.* New York: Pantheon.

Benne, K. S. (1971). Health and marital experience in an urban population. *Journal of Marriage and the Family* 23: 338–50.

Bepko, C. (1989). Disorders of power: Women and addiction in the family. In M. McGoldrick, C. M. Andersen, and F. Walsh, eds., *Women in families: A framework for family therapy* (pp. 406–26). New York: W. W. Norton.

Berne, E. (1972). *What do you say after you say hello? The psychology of human destiny.* New York: Grove.

Bernstein, D. (1993). Female genital anxiety, conflicts, and typical mastery modes. In N. Freedman and B. Distler, eds., *Female identity conflict in clinical practice* (pp. 39–68). Northvale, NJ: Jason Aronson.

Bernstein, D., & Freedman, N. (1993). Gender-specific attribution of identity. In N. Freedman and B. Distler, eds., *Female identity conflict in clinical practice* (pp. 1–16). Northvale, NJ: Jason Aronson.

Bernstein, R. J. (1983). *Beyond objectivism and relativism: Science, hermeneutics and praxis.* Philadephia: University of Pennsylvania Press.

Boss, P., and Thorne, B. (1991). Family sociology and family therapy: A feminist linkage. In M. McGoldrick, C. M. Andersen, and F. Walsh, eds., *Women in families: A framework for family therapy* (pp. 78–96). New York: W.W. Norton.

Brassard, M. R., and Gelardo, M. S. (1987). Psychological maltreatment: The unifying construct in child abuse and neglect. *Social Psychology Review* 16: 127–36.

Bricker-Jenkins, M., and Hooyman, N. R. (1989). A feminist world view: Ideological themes from the feminist movement. In M. Bricker-Jenkins and N. J. Hooyman, eds., *Not for women only: Social work practice for a feminist future* (pp. 7–22). Silver Springs, MD: National Association of Social Workers.

Bridenthal, R. (1982). The family: The view from a room of her own. In B. Thorne and M. Yalom, eds., *Rethinking the family: Some feminist questions* (pp. 225–39). New York: Longman.

Broverman, I. K., Broverman, D. M., and Clarkson, F. E. (1970). Sex-role stereotypes and clinical judgments of mental health. *Journal of Consulting and Clinical Psychology* 34: 1–7.

Brown, G.W., Andrews, B., Harris, T., Adler, Z., and Bridge, L. (1986). Social support, self-esteem and depression. *Psychological Medicine* 16: 813–31.

Brown, L. M., and Gilligan, C. (1992). *Meeting at the crossroads: Women's psychology and girls' development.* Cambridge: Harvard University Press.

Bruner, E. (1986). Ethnography as narrative. In V. Turner and E. Bruner, eds., *The anthropology of experience* (pp. 139–58). Chicago: University of Illinois Press.

Bruner, J. (1990). *Acts of meaning.* Cambridge: Harvard University Press.

Burman, B., and Margolin, G. (1992). Analysis of the association between marital relationships and health problems: An interactional perspective. *Psychological Bulletin* 112: 39–63.

Burstow, B. (1992). *Radical feminist therapy: Working in the context of violence.* Newbury Park, CA: Sage.

Butler, J. B. (1990). *Gender trouble: Feminism and the subversion of identity.* New York: Routledge.

Carlock, C. J., and Martin, P. Y. (1977). Sex composition and the intensive group experience. *Social Work* 22: 27–33.

Chang, V. N. (1994). A study of psychological abuse of women in marriage. *Dissertation Abstracts International* 54: 4258a.

Chang, V. N., and James, M. (1987). Anxiety and projection as related to games and scripts. *Transactional Analysis Journal* 17 (4): 178–84.

Chernin, K. (1981). *The obsession: Reflections on the tyranny of slenderness.* New York: Harper & Row.

Chodorow, N. (1989). *Feminism and psychoanalytic theory.* New Haven, CT: Yale University Press.

Cleek, M. G., and Pearson, T. A. (1985). Perceived causes of divorce: An analysis of interrelationships. *Journal of Marriage and the Family* 47 (1): 179–83.

Cohen, S., Tyrrell, D. A., and Smith, A. P. (1993). Negative life events, perceived stress, negative affect, and susceptibility to the common cold. *Journal of Personality and Social Psychology* 64 (1): 131–40.

Coleman, D. H., and Straus, M. A. (1986). Marital power, conflict, and violence in a nationally representative sample of American couples. *Violence and Victims* 1: 141–57.

Collier, J., Rosaldo, M., and Yanagisako, S. (1982). Is there a family? New anthropological views. In B. Thorne and M. Yalom, eds., *Rethinking the family: Some feminist questions* (pp. 25–39). New York: Longman.

Coltheart, L. (1986). Desire, consent and liberal theory. In C. Pateman and E. Gross, eds., *Feminist challenges* (pp. 112–23). Boston: Northeastern University Press.

Connor, S. (1990). *Postmodernist culture.* Oxford: Basil Blackwell.

Coward, R. (1984). *Female desire.* London: Paladin.

Davis, B. (1992). Women's subjectivity and feminist stories. In L. Ellis and M. G. Flaherty, eds., *Investigating subjectivity: Research on lived experiences* (pp. 53–78). Newbury Park, CA: Sage.

Davis, L. V. (1991). Violence and families. *Social Work* 36 (5): 371–73.

deBeauvoir, S. (1961). *The second sex.* New York: Bantam.

DeGregoria, B. (1987). Sex role attitude and perception of psychological abuse. *Sex Roles* 16 (5/6): 227–35.

Denzin, N. K. (1984). *On understanding emotion.* San Francisco: Jossey-Bass.

———. (1985). On the phenomenology of sexuality, desire, and violence. *Current Perspectives in Social Theory* 6: 39–56.

———. (1987). *The recovering alcoholic.* Newbury Park, CA: Sage.

———. (1988). Action, language, and self in symbolic interactionist thought. *Studies in Symbolic Interaction* 9: 51–80.

———. (1989a). *Interpretative interactionism.* Newbury Park, CA: Sage.

———. (1989b). *The research act.* Englewood Cliffs, NJ: Prentice-Hall.

———. (1991a). Empiricist cultural studies in America: A deconstructive reading. *Current Perspectives in Social Theory* 11: 17–39.

———. (1991b). *Images of postmodern society: Social theory and contemporary cinema.* Newbury Park, CA: Sage.

Dinnerstein, D. (1976). *The mermaid and the minotaur: Sexual arrangements and human malaise.* New York: Harper & Row.

Dobash, R. E., and Dobash, R. (1979). *Violence against wives: A case against the patriarchy.* New York: Free Press.

Dominelli, L., and McLeod, E. (1989). *Feminist social work.* London: Macmillan.

Ehrenreich B., and English, D. (1978). *For her own good: 150 years of advice to women.* New York: Doubleday/Anchor.

Engels, B. (1990). *The emotionally abused woman: Overcoming destructive patterns and reclaiming yourself.* New York: Fawcett Columbine.

Evans, P. (1992). *The verbally abusive relationship: How to recognize it and how to respond.* Holbrook, MA: Bob Adams.

Ewart, C. K., Taylor, C. B., Kraemer, H. C., and Agras, W. S. (1991). High blood pressure and marital discord: Not being nasty matters more than being nice. *Health Psychology* 10: 155–63.

Felman, S. (1977). To open the question. *Yale French Studies* 55–56: 5–10.

Ferraro, K. J. (1979). Physical and emotional battering: Aspects of managing hurt. *California Sociologist* 2 (2): 134–49.

———. (1988). An existential approach to battering. In G. T. Hotaling, D. Finkelhor, J. T. Kirkpatrick, and M. A. Straus, eds., *Family abuse and its consequences* (pp. 126–36). Newbury Park, CA: Sage.

Ferraro, K. J., and Johnson, J. M. (1983). How women experience battering: The process of victimization. *Social Problems* 30 (3): 325–39.

Ferree, M. M. (1990). Beyond separate spheres: Feminism and family research. *Journal of Marriage and the Family* 52: 866–84.

Flax, J. (1990a). Postmodernism and gender relations in feminist theory. In L. Nicholson, ed., *Feminism/Postmodernism* (pp. 39–62). New York: Routledge.

————. (1990b). *Thinking fragments: Psychoanalysis, feminism, and postmodernism in the contemporary West*. Berkeley: University of California Press.

Follingstad, D. R. (1980). A reconceptualization of issues in the treatment of abused women: A case study. *Psychotherapy: Theory, Research and Practice* 17 (3): 294–303.

Follingstad, D. R., Rutledge, L. L., Berg, B. J., Hause, E. S., and Polek, D. S. (1990). The role of emotional abuse in physically abusive relationships. *Journal of Family Violence*: 5: 107–120.

Forward, S. (1986). *Men who hate women and the women who love them*. New York: Bantam.

Foucault, M. (1980). *Power/knowledge: Selected interviews and other writings*. New York: Pantheon.

Fraser, N. (1991). The uses and abuses of French discourse theories for feminist politics. In P. Wexler, ed., *Critical theory now* (pp. 98–117). New York: Falmer.

Friedan, B. (1963). *The feminine mystique*. New York: Norton.

Gallant, J. P. (1993). New ideas for the school social worker in the counseling of children and families. *Social Work in Education* 15 (2): 119–26.

Gallop, J. (1982). *The daughter's seduction: Feminism and psychoanalysis*. Ithaca, NY: Cornell University Press.

————. (1985). *Reading Lacan*. Ithaca, NY: Cornell University Press.

Gardiner, J. K. (1985). Mind mother: Psychoanalysis and feminism. In G. Greene and C. Kahn, eds., *Making a difference: Feminist literary criticism* (pp. 113–45). London: Methuen.

Gelb, J. (1983). The politics of wife abuse. In I. Diamond, ed., *Families, politics, and public policy: A feminist dialogue on women and the state* (pp. 250–62). New York: Longman.

Gelles, R. J. (1976). Abused wives: Why do they stay? *Journal of Marriage and the Family* 38: 659–68.

Gelles, R. J., and Cornell, C. P. (1990). *Intimate violence in families* (2d ed.). Newbury Park, CA: Sage.

Gergen, M. M. (1992). Life stories: Pieces of a dream. In G. Rosenwald and R. Ochberg, eds., *Storied lives* (pp. 127–44). New Haven, CT: Yale University Press.

Gergen, M. M., and Gergen, K. J. (1983). Narratives of self. In T. R.

Sarbin and K. E. Scheibe, eds., *Studies in social identity* (pp. 254–73). New York: Praeger.

———. (1984). The social construction of narrative accounts. In K. J. Gergen and M. M. Gergen, eds., *Historical social psychology* (pp. 173–210). Hillsdale, II: Lawrence Erlbaum.

Giddens, A. (1987). Structuralism, post-structuralism and the production of culture. In A. Giddens and J. H. Turner, eds., *Social theory today* (pp. 195–223). Stanford, CA: Stanford University Press.

Gilligan, C. (1982). *In a different voice: Psychological theory and women's development.* Cambridge: Harvard University Press.

Glaser B. G., and Strauss, A. (1967). *The discovery of grounded research: Strategies for qualitative research.* New York: De Gruyter.

Goffman, E. (1974). *Frame analysis.* New York: Harper.

———. (1977). The arrangement between the sexes. *Theory and Society* 4 (3): 301–33.

Gondolf, E. (1987). Evaluating programs for men who batter: Problems and perspectives. *Journal of Family Violence* 2: 95–108.

Goodrich, T. J., Rampage, C., Ellman, B., and Halstead, K. (1988). *Feminist family therapy: A casebook.* New York: W. W. Norton.

Graham, D. L. R., Rawlings, E., and Rimini, N. (1988). Survivors of terror—battered women, hostages and the Stockholm Syndrome. In K. Yllö and M. Bogard, eds., *Feminist perspectives on wife abuse* (pp. 217–33). Newbury Park, CA: Sage.

Grosz, E. (1990). *Jacques Lacan: A feminist introduction.* London: Routledge.

Guba, E. G. (1990). Subjectivity and objectivity. In E. W. Eisner and A. Peshkin, eds., *Qualitative inquiry in education* (pp. 74–91). New York: Teacher's College Press.

Hanmer, J., and Maynard, M. (1987). *Women, violence, and social control.* Atlantic Highlands, NY: Humanities.

Harding, S. (1991). *Whose science? Whose knowledge? Thinking for women's lives.* Ithaca, NY: Cornell University Press.

Hare-Mustin, R. T. (1991). The problem of gender in family therapy theory. In M. McGoldrick, C. M. Anderson, and F. Walsh, eds., *Women in families: A Framework for family therapy* (pp. 61–77). New York: W. W. Norton.

Hart, S. N., & Brassard, M. R. (1987). A major threat to children's mental health: Psychological maltreatment. *American Psychologist* 42: 160–65.

Hartmann, H. (1976). Capitalism, patriarchy, and job discrimination by sex. In M. Blaxall and B. Reagan, eds., *Women and the work place* (pp. 137–69). Chicago: University of Chicago Press.

Henson, D. M., and Schinderman, J. L. (1981). Therapy with battered women. In A. Weick and S. T. Vandiver, eds., *Women, power, and change* (pp. 27–37). Washington, DC: National Association of Social Workers.

Herman, J. L. (1992). *Trauma and recovery: The aftermath of violence—from domestic abuse to political terror.* New York: Basic Books.

Hochschild, A. R. (1990). Ideology and emotion management: A perspective and path for future research. In T. D. Kemper, ed., *Research agenda in the sociology of emotions* (pp. 117–42). Albany, NY: State University of New York Press.

Hoffman, P. (1984). Psychological abuse of women by spouses and live-in lovers. *Women and Therapy* 3 (1): 34–47.

Horner, A. (1986). *Being and loving.* Northvale, NJ: Jason Aronson.

Horney, K. (1937). *The neurotic personality of our time.* New York: Norton.

Hudson, W., and McIntosh, S. (1981). The assessment of spouse abuse: Two quantifiable dimensions. *Journal of Marriage and the Family* 43: 873–85.

Hyatt, L. (1995). "An old story retold." Unpublished poem.

Hyden, M. (1994). Woman battering as a marital act: Interviewing and analysis in context. In C. K. Riessman, ed., *Qualitative studies in social work research* (pp. 95–112). Thousand Oaks, CA: Sage.

Irigaray, L. (1985a). *Speculum of the other woman.* Ithaca, NY: Cornell University Press.

———. (1985b). *This sex which is not one.* Ithaca, NY: Cornell University Press.

Jack, D. C. (1991). *Silencing the self: Women and depression.* Cambridge: Harvard University Press.

Johnson, M. (1976). An approach to feminist therapy. *Psychotherapy: Theory, Research and Practice* 13: 245–65.

Jones, A., and Schechter, S. (1992). *When love goes wrong.* New York: HarperCollins.

Kaplan, A.G. (1984). The "self-in-relation": Implications for depression in women. Wellesley, MA: Stone Center Working Papers Series, paper #14.

Kaschak, E. (1992). *Engendered lives: A new psychology of women's experience.* New York: Basic Books.

Kellner, D. (1989). *Critical theory, Marxism, and modernity.* Baltimore, MD: Johns Hopkins University Press.

Kiecolt-Glaser, J. K., Fisher, L. D., Ogrocki, P., Stout, J. C., Speicher, C. E., and Glaser, R. (1987). Marital quality, marital disruption, and immune function. *Psychosomatic Medicine* 49 (1); 13–34.

Kiecolt-Glaser, J. K., and Glaser, R. (1991). Psychosocial factors, stress, disease, and immunity. In R. Ader, D. L. Felten, and N. Cohen, eds., *Psychoneuroimmunology* (pp. 849–67). San Diego, CA: Academic.

Kiecolt-Glaser, J. K., Kennedy, S., Malkoff, S., Fisher, L., Speicher, C. E., and Glaser, R. (1988). Marital discord and immunity in males. *Psychosomatic Medicine* 50: 213–29.

Kiecolt-Glaser, J. K., Malarkey, W. B., Chee, M., Newton, T., Cacioppo, J. T., Mao, H., and Glaser, R. (1993). Negative behavior during marital conflict is associated with immunological down-regulation. *Psychosomatic Medicine* 55: 395–409.

Kieffer, C. H. (1984). Citizen empowerment: A developmental perspective. *Prevention in Human Services* 3: 9–36.

Koslof, C. H. (1984). The battered woman: A developmental perspective. *Smith College Studies in Social Work* 54 (3): 181–203.

Kosof, A. (1985). *Incest*. New York: Watts.

Kravetz, D. (1986). Women and mental health. In N. Van Den Bergh and L. Cooper, eds., *Feminist visions for social work* (pp. 101–27). Silver Springs, MD: National Association of Social Workers.

Kreman, E. (1980). The social work profession encounters the battered woman. In E. Norman and A. Mancuso, eds., *Women's issues and social work practice* (pp. 113–32). Itasca, Il: F. E. Peacock.

Kurz, D. (1989). Social science perspectives on wife abuse: Current debates and future directions. *Gender and Society* 3: 489–505.

Lacan, J. (1977). *Ecrits: A selection*. A. Sheridan, trans. New York: Norton.

Laird, J. (1991a). Enactments of power through ritual. In T. J. Goodrich, ed., *Women and power: Perspectives for family therapy* (pp. 123–47). New York: W. W. Norton.

————. (1991b). Women and stories: Restorying women's self-constructions. In M. McGoldrick, C. M. Anderson, and F. Walsh, eds., *Women in families: A framework for family therapy*, (pp. 427–50). New York: W. W. Norton.

Langman, L. (1991). From pathos to panic: American character meets the future. In P. Wexler, ed., *Critical theory now* (pp. 165–241). London: Falmer Press.

Lazarus, R. S., and Folkman, S. (1984). *Stress, appraisal, and coping*. New York: Springer.

Lyotard, J. F. (1986). *The postmodern condition: A report on knowledge*. Manchester, UK: Manchester University Press.

MacIntyre, A. (1981). *After virtue*. Notre Dame, IN: University of Notre Dame Press.

Martin, D. (1976). *Battered wives*. New York: Pocket Books.

Massey, R. F. (1989). Integrating systems theory and TA in couples therapy. *Transactional Analysis Journal* 19 (3): 128–36.

McAdams, D. P. (1988). *Power, intimacy, and the life story: Personological inquiries into identity.* New York: Guilford.

————. (1993). *Stories we live by: Personal myths and the making of the self.* New York: William Morrow.

McGrath, C. (1979). The crisis of domestic violence. *Socialist Review* 43: 7–25.

Miller, J. B. (1976). *Toward a new psychology of women.* Boston: Beacon Press.

————. (1991). Women and power. In J. V. Jordan, A. G. Kaplan, J. B. Miller, I. P. Stiver, and J. L. Surrey, eds., *Women's growth in connection: Writings from the Stone Center* (pp. 197–205). New York: Guilford.

Minnich, E. K. (1990). *Transforming knowledge.* Philadephia, PA: Temple University Press.

Mishler, E. G. (1986). The analysis of interview-narratives. In T. R. Sarbin, ed., *Narrative psychology: The storied nature of human conduct* (pp. 233–55). New York: Praeger.

Mitchell, J. (1966). Women: The longest revolution. *New Left Review* 40: 11–37.

Moi, T. (1985). *Sexual/textual politics: Feminist literary theory.* London: Routledge.

Money, J. (1973). Gender role, gender identity, core gender identity: Usage and definition of terms. *Journal of the American Academy of Psychoanalysis* 1: 397–402.

Money, J., and Erhardt, A. A. (1972). *Man and woman: Boy and girl.* Baltimore, MD: Johns Hopkins University Press.

Moore, D. M. (1979). *Battered women.* Beverly Hills, CA: Sage.

Murphy, C. M., and Casardi, M. (1993). Psychological aggression and abuse in marriage. In R. L. Hampton, T. P. Gullotta, G. R. Adams, E. H. Potter, and R. P. Weissberg, eds., *Family violence: Prevention and treatment* (pp. 86–112). Newbury Park, CA: Sage.

Nesbit, W. C., and Karagianis, L. D. (1987). Psychological abuse in the home and in the school. *Canadian Journal of Education* 12 (1): 177–83.

Nicarthy, G. (1986). *Getting free: A handbook for women in abusive relationships.* 2d ed. Seattle, WA: Seal.

Nodding, N. (1984). *Caring: A feminine approach to ethics and moral education.* Berkeley: University of California Press.

Norman, E. (1980). Sex roles and sexism. In E. Norman and A. Mancuso, eds., *Women's issues and social work practice* (pp. 11–20). Itasca, IL: F. E. Peacock.

Norman, E., and Mancuso, A., eds. (1980). *Women's issues and social work practice*. Itasca, IL: F. E. Peacock.

Novey, T., and Novey, P. (1983). Don't make daddy mad or teaching women how to negotiate with men. *Transactional Analysis Journal* 13 (2): 97–103.

Oakley, A. (1981). Interviewing women: A contradiction in terms. In H. Roberts, ed., *Doing feminist research* (pp. 30–61). Boston: Routledge & Kegan Paul.

O'Brien, M. (1981). Feminist theory and dialectical logic. In N. O. Keohane, M. Z. Rosaldo, and B. C. Gelpi, eds., *Feminist theory: A critique of ideology* (pp. 99–112). Chicago: University of Chicago Press.

Orbach, S. (1978). *Fat is a feminist issue.* New York: Paddington.

Pagelow, M. (1981). *Woman-battering.* Beverly Hills, CA: Sage.

Personal Narratives Group, eds., (1989). *Interpreting women's lives: Feminist theory and personal narratives.* Bloomington: Indiana University Press.

Pfouts, J. (1978). Violent families: Coping responses of abused wives. *Child Welfare* 57: 101–111.

Pizzey, E. (1974). *Scream quietly or the neighbors will hear.* Baltimore, MD: Penguin.

Polkinghorne, D. E. (1988). *Narrative knowing and the human sciences.* Albany: State University of New York Press.

Pozatek, E. (1994). The problem of certainty: Clinical social work in the postmodern era. *Social Work* 39 (4): 396–404.

Ptacek, J. (1988). Why do men batter their wives? In K. Yllö and M. Bogard, eds., *Feminist perspectives on wife abuse* (pp. 133–57). Newbury Park, CA: Sage.

Rappaport, J. (1981). In praise of paradox: A social policy of empowerment over prevention. *American Journal of Community Psychology* 9: 1–25.

Raymond, B., and Bruschi, I. G. (1989). Psychological abuse among college women in dating relationships. *Perceptual and Motor Skills* 69: 1283–97.

Reinharz, S. (1979). *On becoming a social scientist: From survey research and participant observation to experiential analysis.* San Francisco: Jossey-Bass.

Riessman, C. (1990). *Divorce talk: Women and men make sense of personal relationships.* New Brunswick, NJ: Rutgers University Press.

Robinson, J. A., and Hawpe, L. (1986). Narrative thinking as a heuristic process. In T. R. Sarbin, ed., *Narrative psychology: The storied nature of human conduct* (pp. 111–128). New York: Praeger.

Rounsaville, B. (1978). Theories in marital violence: Evidence from a study of battered women. *Victimology* 3 (1–2): 11–31.

Rubin, G. (1975). The traffic in women: Notes on the "political economy" of sex. In R. R. Reiter, ed., *Toward an anthropology of women* (pp. 157–210). New York: Monthly Review Press.

Rubin, L. B. (1981). Sociological research: The subjective dimension. *Symbolic Interactionism* 4 (1): 42–57.

Rukeyer, M. (1994). *A Muriel Rukeyer reader.* (Ed. J. H. Levi). New York: Norton.

Saleeby, D. (1994). Culture, theory, and narrative: The intersection of meanings in practice. *Social Work* 39 (4): 351–61.

Sarbin, T. R. (1986). The narrative as a root metaphor for psychology. In T. R. Sarbin, ed., *Narrative psychology: The storied nature of human conduct* (pp. 3–21). New York: Praeger.

Sartre, J. P. (1966). *Being and nothingness: An essay in phenomenological ontology.* Translated by H. E. Barnes. New York: Citadel Press.

———. (1981). *The family idiot: Gustav Flaubert, 1821–1857.* Vol. 1. Chicago: University of Chicago Press.

Sattel, J. W. (1983). Men, inexpressiveness, and power. In L. Richardson and V. Taylor, ed., *Feminist frontiers: Rethinking sex, gender, and society* (pp. 242–46). New York: Random House.

Scanzoni, J. (1972). *Sexual bargaining.* Englewood Cliffs, NJ: Prentice-Hall.

Schechter, S. (1982). *Women and male violence.* Boston: South End.

Schechter, S., and Gary, L. (1988). A framework for understanding and empowering battered women. In M. Straus, ed., *Abuse and victimization across the life span* (pp. 240–53). Baltimore: Johns Hopkins University Press.

Schiff, J. L. (1975). *Cathexis reader: Transactional analysis treatment of psychosis.* New York: Harper & Row.

Schubert-Walker, L. J. (1981). Are women's groups different? *Psychotherapy: Theory, Research, and Practice* 18: 240–45.

Schwendinger, J. R., and Schwendinger, H. (1983). *Rape and inequality.* Beverly Hills, CA: Sage.

Seligman, M. E. (1975). *Helplessness: On depression, development, and death.* San Francisco: W. H. Freeman.

Shepard, M. (1991). Feminist practice principles for social work intervention in wife abuse. *Affilia* 6 (2): 87–93.

Shepard, M., and Pence, E. (1988). The effect of battering on the employment status of women. *Affilia* 3 (2): 55–61.

Smart, B. (1990). Modernity, postmodernity and the present. In B. S. Turner, ed., *Theories of modernity and postmodernity* (pp. 14–30). London: Sage.

Smith, M. D. (1990). Patriarchal ideology and wife beating: A test of a feminist hypothesis. *Violence and Victims* 5 (4): 257–73.

Sonkin, D. J., Martin, D., and Walker, L. E. (1985). *The male batterer.* New York: Springer.

Stanley, L., & Wise, S. (1983). *Breaking out: Feminist consciousness and feminist research.* London: Routledge & Kegan Paul.

Stets, J. E. (1991). Psychological aggression in dating relationships: The role of interpersonal control. *Journal of Family Violence* 6 (1): 97–114.

Straus, M. A. (1977). A sociological perspective on the prevention and treatment of wifebeating. In M. Roy, ed., *Battered women* (pp. 194–238). New York: Van Nostrand Reinhold.

———. (1979). Measuring intrafamily conflict and violence: The Conflict Tactics Scales. *Journal of Marriage and the Family* 41: 75–88.

Straus, M. A., Golles, R. J., and Steinmetz, S. K. (1980). *Behind closed doors: Violence in the American family.* Garden City, NY: Doubleday.

Sullivan, H. S. (1953). *The interpersonal theory of psychiatry.* New York: Norton.

Swerdow, A., ed. (1978). *Feminist perspectives on housework and child care.* Bronxville, NY: Sarah Lawrence College Press.

Symonds, A. (1979). Violence against women: The myth of masochism. *American Journal of Psychotherapy* 33 (2): 161–73.

Tavris, C. (1992). *The mismeasure of woman: Why women are not the better sex, the inferior sex, or the opposite sex.* New York: Simon & Schuster.

Telch, C. F., and Lindquist, C. U. (1984). Violent versus non-violent couples: A comparison of patterns. *Psychotherapy* 21: 242–48.

Thorne, B. (1982). Feminist rethinking of the family: An overview. In B. Thorne and M. Yalom, eds., *Rethinking the family: Some feminist questions* (pp. 1–24). New York: Longman.

Tolman, R. M. (1989). The development of a measure of psychological maltreatment of women by their male partners. *Violence and Victims* 4 (3): 159–77.

———. (1992). Psychological abuse of women. In R. T. Ammerman and M. Hersen, eds., *Assessment of family violence: A clinical and legal sourcebook* (pp. 291–310). New York: Wiley.

Turner, S. F., and Shapiro, C. H. (1986). Battered women: Mourning the death of a relationship. *Social Work* 31 (5): 372–76.

Van Den Bergh, N., and Cooper, L. (1986). Introduction. In N. Van Den

Bergh and L. Cooper, eds., *Feminist visions for social work* (pp. 1–25). Silver Springs, MD: National Association of Social Workers.

Walker, L. E. (1979). *The battered woman*. New York: Harper & Row.

———. (1984). *The battered woman syndrome*. New York: Springer.

Walters, M., Carter, B., Papp, P., & Silverstein, O. (1988). Toward a feminist perspective in family therapy. In M. Walters, B. Carter, P. Papp, and O. Silverstein, eds., *The invisible web: Gender patterns in family relationships* (pp. 15–30). New York: Guilford.

Weedon, C. (1987). *Feminist practice and poststructuralist theory*. New York: Basil Blackwell.

Weissman, M. (1987). Advances in psychiatric epidemiology: Rates and risks for major depression. *American Journal of Public Health* 77: 445–51.

Wetzel, J. W. (1981). Redefining mental health. In A. Weick and S. T. Vandiver, eds., *Women, power, and change* (pp. 3–16). Washington, DC: National Association of Social Workers.

White, M., and Epston, D. (1990). *Narrative means to therapeutic ends*. New York: Norton.

Woolf, V. [1942] (1970). Professions for women. In *The death of the moth and other essays*. New York: Harcourt Brace Jovanovich.

Yllö, K. (1983). Using a feminist approach in quantitative research: A case study. In C. Finkelhor, R. J. Gelles, G. T. Hotaling, and M. A. Straus, eds., *The dark side of families: Current family violence research* (pp. 277–88). Beverly Hills, CA: Sage.

———. (1984). The status of women, marital equality, and violence against wives. *Journal of Family Issues* 5: 307–20.

———. (1993). Through a feminist lens: Gender, power, and violence. In R. J. Gelles and D. R. Loseke, eds., *Current controversies on family violence* (pp. 47–62). Newbury Park, CA: Sage.

Yllö, K., and Straus, M. A. (1984). Patriarchy and violence against wives: The impact of structural and normative factors. *Journal of International and Comparative Social Welfare* 1: 1–13.

Young, I. M. (1990a). *Justice and the politics of difference*. Princeton, NJ: Princeton University Press.

———. (1990b). *Throwing like a girl and other essays in feminist philosophy and social theory*. Bloomington: Indiana University Press.

Zimmerman, M. A. (1990). Toward a theory of learned hopefulness: A structural modal analysis of participation and empowerment. *Journal of Research in Personality* 24: 71–86.

Zimmerman, M. A., and Rappaport, J. (1988). Citizen participation, perceived control, and psychological empowerment. *American Journal of Community Psychology* 16: 725–50.

INDEX

About the Author

VALERIE NASH CHANG is an Associate Professor at the Indiana University School of Social Work. She has practiced psychology for 25 years and has been actively involved in training psychotherapists.

ISBN 0-275-95209-6

EAN

9 780275 952099

HARDCOVER BAR CODE